Advances
in
Science
and
Technology
in
the USSR

Technology Series

ADVANCES IN
SCIENCE AND TECHNOLOGY
IN THE USSR

Computer-Aided Design of Language Processors

V. SHANGIN and P. TIMOFEEV

Translated from the Russian by O. Belonogova

Mir Publishers

Moscow

CRC Press

Boca Raton   Ann Arbor   London

Library of Congress Cataloging-in-Publication Data

Shangin V. F.
    Computer-aided design of language processors / V. Shangin and P. Timofeev ; translated from the Russian by O. Belonogova.
        p.   cm. - - (Advances in science and technology in the USSR)
    Includes bibliographical references and index.
    ISBN 0-8493-7537-1
    1. Translators (Computer programs) 2. Computer-aided software engineering. 3. Programming languages (Electronic computers)
    I. Timofeev, P. II. Title. III. Series.
QA76.76.T83S53   1991
005.4´5—dc20   91-38349
                                                                                                     CIP

    Direct all inquiries to CRC Press, Inc., 2000 Corporate Blvd., N.W., Boca Raton, Florida, 33431.

© 1992 by CRC Press, Inc.

International Standard Book Number 0-8493-7537-1
Library of Congress Card Number 91-38349

Printed in the United States   1 2 3 4 5 6 7 8 9 0

CONTENTS

6   Contents

INTRODUCTION

Computer-aided design of language processors ensures higher efficiency in creating compilers, interpreters, macrogenerators, cross and resident programming systems and software for flexible industrial systems. It also promotes solution of a number of problems on improving software and applying computers in industry.

Most languages described mainly result from the development of syntax-oriented translators for various programming languages. The advent of the first more or less complicated languages required formalizing techniques and mathematic tools. The former usually concerned context-free syntactic properties of a language. It is more difficult to specify the properties intended to reveal the sense of language constructs. Among the well-known methods of describing syntax and semantics, the systems of productions, attribute grammers and Viennese metalanguage enjoy the most common use.

Using formal description to obtain automatically the matching language identifier is of special interest. Presented in the literature the methods and systems for constructing translators according to formal grammar description render process of syntax analyzers for context-free languages automatic. For example, the YET ANOTHER COMPILER-COMPILER (YACC) system produces the push-down automaton; the compiler generator XPL produces tables of parsing algorithm for mixed strategy precedence; DELTA, SDELTA, SUPER produces LR-parsers. These systems represent language semantics in the form of attributes and operations on them recorded either in programming language, such as the C-language for the YACC system, or in some special language. Systems intended for constructing translators reside usually on mainframes or minicomputers.

However, the existing methods consider, as a rule, certain classes of context-free languages and uniprocessor parsing. Besides, by these methods the sentence parsing may be other than non-searching one. At the same time, non-searching techniques do not present the principles of automatic conversion of formal language description into syntax analyzer. The methods applied either exclude semantics or face certain difficulties in relating syntax to semantics. So there are practically no deterministic methods described, which enable parsing all the variety of formal languages.

The book presents the well-grounded technique of non-reset parsing of both context-free and context-sensitive formal languages for uniprocessor and multiprocessor systems. It also describes a version of the language processor generator for microcomputers, which is based on the abovementioned technique and implemented as an extention of Pascal and Macroassembler. The

CAD toolkits for representing the generator in other programming languages are also included.

Chapter 1 acquaints the reader with the basic terms and definitions of the formal language theory. It classifies formal grammars and shows how to specify language processors. Special emphasis is placed on a thorough analysis of oriented graphs. Some methods of parsing formal languages are also discussed and requests and restrictions imposed on formal grammars, inherent in the methods considered, are noted. Then the book emphasizes the relation between syntax and semantics of languages.

Chapter 2 represents the language processors in terms of loaded oriented graphs and shows how to graph formal grammars. We suggest you toolkits developed to reduce a graph to its deterministic form and a branch statement for context-free languages.

Taking account of the context, Chapter 3 extends the definition of the statement for context-sensitive languages. We discuss the principles of parallel processing in computer systems and state the problem of parallel parsing the character strings. Proceeding from the examination of graphs given in Chapter 2, we pass from language processors to multiprocessors. The chapter addresses the methods of porting parsers from one computer to another.

Chapter 4 covers the metalanguage describing language processors, its syntax and basic constructs. The possibility of recording semantics in programming language is considered and the techniques of programming the language processors and examples of programs intended for parsing are given.

Chapter 5 discusses the intended employment and structure of a language processor generator. It provides its operation algorithms and technical data. The chapter considers an implementation of a generator on microcomputer as an extention of Pascal and Macroassembler. It also discusses a possible implementation of the generator in developing different programming systems.

1 Formal Languages and Language Processors

To acquaint the reader with the notation used in the book and to clarify its content, the chapter gives a brief overview of the concepts and statements accepted in the set theory and the theory of formal languages. Also, we give classifications of formal grammars, some of their types and methods of parsing. Much attention is paid to the application of loaded oriented graphs and interrelationship between syntax and semantics of languages.

1.1. Terms and Definitions

1.1.1. Sets

A set is a collection of different objects. Objects denoted by their names are called *elements*. If a set contains a finite number of elements, it can be designated simply by listing the names of objects. For instance, a set of colours can be specified as

$$C = \{\text{RED, ORANGE, YELLOW, GREEN,}$$
$$\text{BLUE, DARK-BLUE, VIOLET}\}$$

The set C contains seven elements separated by comma and enclosed in braces. The order of listing the elements of the set is arbitrary.

If an object m belongs to C, then m is an element of the set C, i.e.

$$m \in C$$

If m is not the element of C, then this is expressed as

$$m \notin C$$

For instance,

$$\text{ORANGE} \in C, \text{ BROWN} \notin C$$

A set can be designated by simple listing, if it contains a finite number of elements. To constitute an infinite set, objects should possess some common trait. Then, each object will belong to the given set. This common trait is expressed in the form of a statement (predicate) containing one or some variables. The predicate can take on any of two values — true or false. Hence the set comprises the elements for which the predicate is true. Proper care should be taken in selecting the predicate because the set to be defined may be non-existent (the Rassel paradox [1]). The Set N of integers can exemplify an infinite set

$$N = \{x \mid x\text{-prime number}\}$$

The variable x takes on the values from the given set and may be an integer.

The set may have no elements (the predicate is false for all the values of variables). Such a set is called *empty*. It is denoted by $\{\}$ or $\varnothing$ symbols. Sets can be the elements of other sets, which are called systems of sets and are expressed as follows:

$$M = \{M_k, \ k \in I_n\}, \text{ where } I_n = \{1, \ 2, \ ..., \ n\}$$

The set A is said to belong to the set B (i.e. $A \subset B$) if each element of A is the element of B. Then the set A is called a *subset* of the set B. If there exists an element $x \in A$ which does not belong to B ($x \notin B$), then A is not a subset of B, $A \not\subset B$. For example,

$$\{a, \ b, \ c, \ m\} \not\subset \{a, \ c, \ b, \ k, \ l\}, \text{ but}$$

$$\{a, \ b, \ c, \ k\} \subset \{a, \ b, \ c, \ k, \ l\}$$

Note that any set — either A or B — contains an empty set. Two sets A and B are called equal, i.e. $A = B$, if $A \subset B$ and $B \subset A$. For example,

$$\{a, \ b, \ c, \ d\} = \{a, \ c, \ b, \ d\}, \text{ but}$$

$$\{a, \ b, \ c, \ k\} \neq \{a, \ b, \ c, \ d\}$$

Thus the sets A and B are equal if they are identical, i.e. they consist of the same elements.

By performing some operations one can generate new sets. The basic operations performed on sets are as follows: union ($\cup$), intersection ($\cap$), subtraction

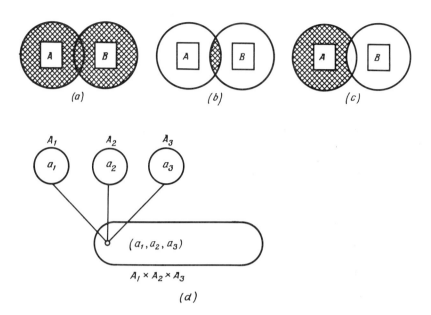

Fig. 1.1. Diagrams for operations on sets: (a) union; (b) intersection; (c) subtraction; and (d) product

($\setminus$), and complement ($'$). Suppose that A and B are the subsets of some universal set: $A \subset U$ and $B \subset U$. Then the basic operations are as follows:

$A \cup B =$ $\{x \mid x \in A \text{ or } x \in B\}$ — union of sets consists of all the elements which belong at least to one of the sets, either A or B

$A \cap B =$ $\{x \mid x \in A \text{ and } x \in B\}$ — intersection of sets consists of all the elements which belong at the same time to both sets A and B

$A \setminus B =$ $\{x \mid x \in A \text{ but } x \notin B\}$ — subtraction of sets consists of all the elements of the set A which are not the elements of the set B

$A' \quad =$ $\{x \mid x \notin A\}$ or $A' = U \setminus A$ — complement consists of all those elements of the set U which are not the elements of the set A

Figure 1.1 (a, b, c) represents the operations on sets in the form of Venn diagrams.

Let us consider some examples of performing operations on the sets $U = \{a, b, c, d, e, f, g, h, q\}$, $A = \{a, b, c, d, e\}$, and $B = \{b, d, h, q\}$:

$$A \cup B = \{a,\ b,\ c,\ d,\ e,\ h,\ q\}$$
$$A \cap B = \{b,\ d\}$$
$$A \setminus B = \{a,\ c,\ e\}$$
$$B \setminus A = \{h,\ q\}$$
$$A' \quad = \{f,\ g,\ h,\ q\}$$

For any sets $A \subset U$, $B \subset U$, $C \subset U$ the following laws are valid [2].

(1) Associative law:

$$(A \cup B) \cup C = A \cup (B \cup C)$$

$$(A \cap B) \cap C = A \cap (B \cap C)$$

(2) Commutative law:

$$A \cup B = B \cup A$$

$$A \cap B = B \cap A$$

(3) Addition:

$$A \cup A' = U$$

$$A \cap A' = \varnothing$$

(4) Idempotential law:

$$A \cup A = A$$

$$A \cap A = A$$

(5) Law of equivalence:

$$A \cup \varnothing = A$$

$$A \cap U = A$$

$$A \cup U = U$$

(6) Law of existence of an empty set:

$$A \cap \varnothing = \varnothing$$

(7) Law of involution:

$$(A')' = A$$

(8) De Morgan's theorem:

$$(A \cup B)' = A' \cap B'$$

$$(A \cap B)' = A' \cup B'$$

(9) Distributive law:

$$A \cup (B \cap C) = (A \cup B) \cap (A \cup C)$$

$$A \cap (B \cup C) = (A \cap B) \cup (A \cap C)$$

Since the sets are associative under union and intersection, these operations can be applied for a sequence of sets, i.e. $A_1, A_2, \ldots, A_n$.

$$A_1 \cup A_2 \cup \ldots \cup A_n \quad \text{or} \quad \bigcup_{i=1}^{n} A_i$$

$$A_1 \cap A_2 \cap \ldots \cap A_n \quad \text{or} \quad \bigcap_{i=1}^{n} A_i$$

The Cartesian product of sets occupies a special place among the operations. The product of the sets A and B, $A \times B$, is the set $\{(a, b) \mid a \in A, b \in B\}$ comprised of arranged pairs of objects. The element of the set A stands first and precedes that of the set B. Consider the following example.

$$\{a, b\} \{1, 2, 3, 4\} = \{(a, 1), (a, 2), (a, 3), (a, 4), (b, 1), (b, 2), (b, 3), (b, 4)\}$$

Note that in the general case $(a, b) \neq (b, a)$, but $\{a, b\} = \{b, a\}$.
The product of three and more sets can be obtained analogously.

$$A_1 \times A_2 \times A_3 = \{(a_1, a_2, a_3) \mid a_1 \in A_1, a_2 \in A_2, a_3 \in A_3\}$$

$$A_1 \times A_2 \times \ldots \times A_n = \{(a_1, a_2, \ldots, a_n) \mid a_1 \in A_1, a_2 \in A_2, \ldots, a_n \in A_n\}$$

In particular, the product of n identical sets

$$A \times A \times \ldots \times A = A^n$$

can be considered.

There are certain interrelationships between the elements of sets. Any subset of the set $A \times B$ is a relation, where the set A is the domain and the set B the range which may be one and the same set. If R is the relation of A to B and $(a, b) \in R$, then it is written as aRb.

The relation R on the set A is called
— *reflexive,* if aRa is valid for all $a \in A$,
— *symmetric,* if from aRb it always follows bRa,
— *transitive,* if from aRb and bRc it always follows aRc.

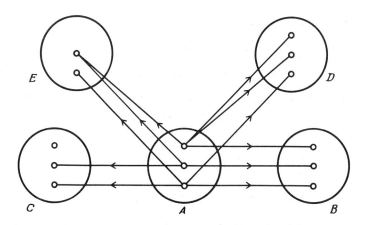

Fig. 1.2. Function properties: $A \to B$, complete one-to-one function; $A \to C$, incomplete function; $A \to D$, not a function; $A \to E$, complete not one-to-one function

Reflexive, symmetric and transitive relations are called the *equivalence relations*. Besides, of importance are the relations known as *mappings* and *functions*.

The function $f : A \to B$ is a relation defined on the set $A \times B$. It is a set of pairs (a, b), where $a \in A$, $b \in B$ and $b = f(a)$. If $(a, b) \in f$ and $(a, c) \in f$, then $b = c$. Such functions are called *unambiguous*. A function defined on all the elements of the set A is called *complete*. The complete function is one-to-one if from $f(a_1) = f(a_2)$, $a_1 \in A$ and $a_2 \in A$ it follows that $a_1 = a_2$.

Figure 1.2 illustrates the properties of mappings stated above. The complete one-to-one mapping $(f : A \to B)$ enables a one-to-one correspondence between the sets A and B.

1.1.2.   Graphs and Trees

Let us examine the set V of dots connected in some way. Let V present the set of vertices, and its elements $v \in V$ the vertices [3]. The *oriented* or *directed graph* $G = (V, E)$ integrates some finite set of vertices and the relation E defined on this set. It can graphically be presented in the following way. Place all the vertices of the set V on a sheet of paper and represent each vertex as a circle in which an element of the V is inscribed. Connect two vertices, i.e. $a \in V$ and $b \in V$, by straight line if the pair $(a, b) \in E$ exists. Thus, the graph G contains the edge (a, b). For example, Figure 1.3 illustrates the graph

$$G_1 = (V_1, E_1), \quad \text{where} \quad V_1 = \{a, b, c, d, e\}$$
$$E_1 = \{(a, b), (b, a), (b, c), (c, d), (c, e), (e, e)\}$$

If the graph contains some sequence of vertices

$$a = v_1, v_2, \ldots, v_n = b$$

where $n \geqslant 0$ and $(v_i, v_{i+1}) \in E$ for $i = 0, 1, \ldots, n - 1$, then it is considered to contain a walk of length n which joins both a and b. If $i = 0$, then $a = b$. The graph $G = (V, E)$ can contain subgraphs of the form $G' = (V', E')$ for $V' \subset V$ and $E' \subset E$. Two subgraphs having no common vertices are called separate subgraphs.

Of interest is a tree — a variety of a graph. The recursive definition of a tree is as follows: A *tree* $T = (V, E)$ is an oriented graph which either has a single vertex called a *root* $T = (\{r\}, \varnothing)$ or is comprised of a root, some

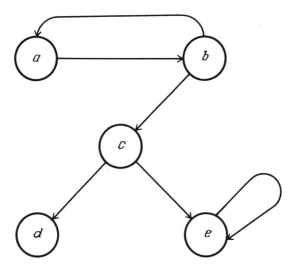

Fig. 1.3. Oriented graph

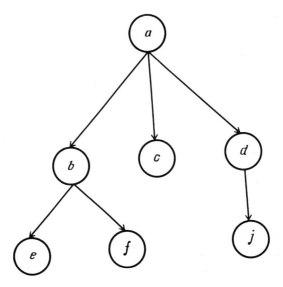

Fig. 1.4. Tree

separate subgraphs-trees, T_1, T_2, ..., T_n, $n > 0$ and edges connecting the root of the tree T and the vertices-roots of the trees T_1, T_2, ..., T_n. Figure 1.4 illustrates a tree. It is usually depicted with its *root* up and the *edges* directed downwards. In this case, it is not necessary to indicate the directions of edges. A vertex with no edges rising from it is called a *leaf*, others are known as inner vertices of a tree.

1.1.3.   Strings

The present book deals with sets whose elements are characters, chains of characters, and strings. A string is a sequence of characters a_1, a_2, ..., a_n each belonging to some finite alphabet A. For instance, the string 10030120 consists of characters from the alphabet {0, 1, 2, 3}. Represent separate characters by lower-case letters a, b, c, d and strings by t, u, v, w, x, y, z. Write a^i for the string containing i characters a. The length of an arbitrary string x is equal to the number of characters in the string and is denoted by $|x|$. For the above example $|10030120| = 8$. In the general case we assume that some empty string x^0 exists and its length is $|x| = 0$. It is denoted by e.

Formally, the strings in the alphabet A are defined as follows [1]:
— e is a string of the alphabet A
— if x is a string of A and $a \in A$, then xa is a string of A
— y is a string if and only if it satisfies the two previous statements

A number of operations can be performed on strings. If x and y are strings, then the string xy is called *concatenation* (chaining or appending) of x and y. Thus, concatenating the string $y = b_1 b_2 \ldots b_n$ to $x = a_1 a_2 \ldots a_m$ yields the string $xy = a_1 a_2 \ldots a_m b_1 b_2 \ldots b_n$. Concatenation is associative but not commutative, hence $(xy) z = x (yz)$ but $xy \neq yx$. For empty strings the statement $ex = xe = x$ is valid for any x. The string $x = a_1 a_2 \ldots a_n$ recorded vice versa, i.e. $x^R = a_n \ldots a_1$, is called inverted.

Let x, y and z be arbitrary strings of some alphabet A and $z = xy$, then x and y are the *prefix* and the *suffix* of the string z, respectively. Thus for the string 10030120 the prefix is represented by e, 1, 10, 100, 1003, 10030, 100301, 1003012, 10030120 and the suffix by e, 0, 20, 120, 0120, 30120, 030120, 0030120, 10030120.

1.1.4. Formal Languages

Let A^* denote the set of strings defined for the alphabet A. For instance, if $A = \{a, b\}$, then

$$A^* = \{e,\ a,\ b,\ aa,\ ab,\ ba,\ bb,\ aaa,\ aab,\ \ldots\}$$

Let A^+ denote the set of all strings of A^* except for e. Thus $A^+ = A^* \setminus \{e\}$.

An arbitrary subset of the set A^* is called a *formal language L* for the alphabet A. Suppose L_1 and L_2 are formal languages. Then their concatenation $L_1 L_2 = \{xy \mid x \in L_1,\ y \in L_2\}$ is a formal language too. For instance, if $L_1 = \{a, 0\}$ and $L_2 = \{e, 0, 10\}$, then $L_1 L_2 = \{a, 0, a0, 00, a10, 010\}$. L^2 denotes two identical formal languages L concatenated one to another. In the general case it is expressed as: $L^0 = \{e\}$, $L^1 = L$, $L^i = LL^{i-1} = L^{i-1}L$ for $i \geqslant 2$. Hence L^* can be determined as $\bigcup\limits_{i=0}^{\infty} L^i$ and $L^+ = L^* \setminus \{e\}$.

1.2. How to Describe Language Processors

1.2.1. Formal Grammars

In Subsection 1.1.4 we have defined a language as a sequence of strings containing characters of some alphabet. To use this language it is necessary to know both syntax and semantics of the language besides the alphabetic characters. By *syntax* is meant syntactic definitions determining exactly the strings valid for the language. These definitions give the rules for constructing words, groups of words, and sentences matching the language, which are composed of alphabetic characters. By *semantics* is meant the rules for interpreting syntactic definitions making the accepted language constructs meaningful. The syntax of programming languages can be described by the Backus-Naur formulas or syntactic diagrams, but the use of formal grammars is universal. Grammar is a mathematical system of generating languages. Its strings are constructed in exact accordance with grammar rules.

The *formal grammar* G represents a quadruple

$$G = (N, \, T, \, P, \, S)$$

Here N is a finite set of *nonterminals*, T is a finite set of *terminals* which does not intersect with N, i.e. $N \cap T = \emptyset$. P is a finite set of rules-productions of the form $v \rightarrow w$, where v and w are respectively the strings of the left-hand part of the production $v \in (N \cup T)^{*+}$ and the right-hand part of the production $w \in (N \cup T)^{*}$. Thus $P \subset \{(v, w) \mid v \in A^{*} \times N \times A^{*}$ and $w \in A^{*}\}$, where $A = N \cup T$ and S is the initial character of the grammar $S \in N$. The symbol $\rightarrow$ appearing in the production $v \rightarrow w$ indicates the possible substitution of w for v. Let us examine the following grammar $G_1 = (\{D, S\}, \{0, 1, 2, 3, 4, 5, 6, 7\}, P, S)$, where the set P contains the following productions:

$$D \rightarrow 0$$
$$D \rightarrow 1$$
$$D \rightarrow 2$$
$$D \rightarrow 3$$
$$D \rightarrow 4$$
$$D \rightarrow 5$$
$$D \rightarrow 6$$
$$D \rightarrow 7$$
$$S \rightarrow D$$
$$S \rightarrow DS$$

The production set notation can be reduced by grouping the productions with similar left-hand parts. The right-hand parts of these productions are written in a line separated by the symbol "|". Now the set of productions of grammar G_1 takes the form:

$$D \to 0 \mid 1 \mid 2 \mid 3 \mid 4 \mid 5 \mid 6 \mid 7$$
$$S \to D \mid DS$$

The grammar recursively defines the generated language which comprises a sequence of strings derived from the initial character. Let us formally define the string derived for the grammar $G = (N, T, P, S)$. The string $x_1 w x_2$ is called *derived*, if $v \to w$ is a production of the set P and $x_1 v x_2 \in (N \cup T)^+$ is a string of terminal and non-terminal characters of the length $\geqslant 1$ [2]. The derived string is obtained by substituting the string w for v in the string $x_1 v x_2$. This transformation is expressed as:

$$x_1 v x_2 \underset{G}{\rightrightarrows} x_1 w x_2$$

The transformation $\underset{G}{\rightrightarrows}$ may be considered as a relation on the set $(N \cup T)^*$ [1, 4]. It is reflexive so far as the string v may be substituted for itself. However it is not valid for all the elements of $(N \cup T)^*$. It is neither transitive nor symmetric.

The relation $\underset{G}{\overset{*}{\rightrightarrows}}$ on the set $(N \cup T)^*$ is specified as $x_1 \underset{G}{\overset{*}{\rightrightarrows}} x_n$, if a sequence $x_1, x_2, \ldots, x_n \in (N \cup T)^*$ for $n \geqslant 1$ exists and $x_1 \underset{G}{\rightrightarrows} x_2 \underset{G}{\rightrightarrows} x_3 \underset{G}{\rightrightarrows} \cdots \underset{G}{\rightrightarrows} x_n$. In this case the string x_n is said to be derived from the string x_1 in one or more steps. The relation $\underset{G}{\overset{*}{\rightrightarrows}}$ is reflexive and transitive but not symmetric. The string $x \in (N \cup T)$ derived from the initial character in the form of the string $(S \underset{G}{\overset{*}{\rightrightarrows}} x)$ is called the *sentential form*. The sentential form containing no nonterminals is called a *sentence*. The collection of all the sentences of the grammar G is called a language *generated by this grammar* and is denoted by $L(G)$. Thus

$$L(G) = \{x \in T^* \mid S \underset{G}{\overset{*}{\rightrightarrows}} x\}$$

Both grammars G and G' may generate the same language $L(G) = L(G')$. Such grammars are considered *equivalent*. Henceforth we will omit the character G in the notations of the form $\underset{G}{\overset{*}{\rightrightarrows}}$ and $\underset{G}{\rightrightarrows}$ if there is no doubt what grammar is discussed.

Consider the examples of sentences in some languages. For the grammar

G_1 described above, the language includes the following sentences which represent octal numbers.

$$
\begin{aligned}
2 \text{ derivation } S \ & \Rightarrow\ D \Rightarrow 2 \\
23 \text{ derivation } S \ & \Rightarrow DS \text{ (rule } S \to DS) \\
& \Rightarrow 2S \text{ (rule } D \to 2) \\
& \Rightarrow 2D \text{ (rule } S \to D) \\
& \Rightarrow 23 \text{ (rule } D \to 3) \\
637 \text{ derivation } S \ & \Rightarrow\ DS \Rightarrow 6S \Rightarrow 6DS \Rightarrow 63S \\
& \Rightarrow 63D \Rightarrow 637
\end{aligned}
$$

The left-hand parts of all the productions of this grammar contain only one character each. The left-hand parts of productions of the next grammar $G_2 = (\{S, B\}, \{a, b\}, P, S)$ contain strings of more than one character.

$$
\begin{aligned}
S &\to aSB \mid aB \\
aB &\to ab \\
bB &\to bb
\end{aligned}
$$

For the grammar G_2, a string of the form $a^n b^n$ $(n \geqslant 1)$ can be derived.

$S \Rightarrow aSB$	(rule $S \to aSB$)
$\Rightarrow aaSBB$	(rule $S \to aSB$)
$\Rightarrow aaaBBB$	(rule $S \to aB$)
$\Rightarrow aaabBB$	(rule $aB \to ab$)
$\Rightarrow aaabbB$	(rule $bB \to bb$)
$\Rightarrow aaabbb$	(rule $bB \to bb$)

1.2.2.   Classification of Grammars

The grammar G may be of four types. It depends either upon the form of its generative rules or the form of both strings v and w in the left- and right-hand parts of productions $v \to w$ from the set P of the grammar

G. The grammar G is called *right linear* or *ATN grammar* (type 3) if $v \in N$, $w \in T \times N$ or $w \in T$, i.e. each rule from the set P is represented as $A \rightarrow xB \mid x$, where $x \in T$ and $\{A, B\} \subset N$. The grammar G is *context-free* (type 2) if $v \in N$, $w \in (T \cup N)^+$. It is *context-sensitive non-abridging* (type 1), if $v \in (T \cup N)^* \times N \times (T \cup N)^*$, $w \in (T \cup N)^*$, and the string v is not longer than the string w, i.e. ($\mid v \mid < \mid w \mid$). The grammar G is called *context-sensitive unrestricted* (type $\varnothing$), if $v \in (T \cup N)^* \times N \times (T \cup N)^*$, $w \in (T \cup N)^*$.

A language generated by some grammar of the type n is called a language of the type n. Thus the language $L(G_1)$ generated by the grammar G_1 is context-free and $L(G_2)$ is context-sensitive of type 1. Let us examine two more grammars generating identifiers of a programming language, where the letter stands first followed by the integer. The first grammar ($\{S, D\}$, $\{a, 0, 1, 2, 3, 4, 5, 6, 7, 8, 9\}$, P, S) is right linear and contains the following productions:

$$S \rightarrow a \mid aD$$
$$D \rightarrow 0 \mid 1 \mid 2 \mid 3 \mid 4 \mid 5 \mid 6 \mid 7 \mid 8 \mid 9 \mid 0D \mid 1D \mid$$
$$2D \mid 3D \mid 4D \mid 5D \mid 6D \mid 7D \mid 8D \mid 9D$$

Though the second grammar specifies the same set of identifiers, it is a context-free grammar. Its productions are

$$S \rightarrow a \mid aD$$
$$F \rightarrow 0 \mid 1 \mid 2 \mid 3 \mid 4 \mid 5 \mid 6 \mid 7 \mid 8 \mid 9$$
$$D \rightarrow F \mid DF$$

This grammar includes an additional nonterminal character F to designate digits. The language generated by both grammars is represented by the set

$$\{a\} \times \{0, 1, 2, 3, 4, 5, 6, 7, 8, 9\}^+$$

The four types of languages and grammars defined above comply with the *Homsky hierarchy*. By the above definition, the context-free grammar does not accept the so-called *e*-productions of the form $A \rightarrow e$. Nevertheless some authors consider *e*-productions acceptable, and call context-free grammars, if they do not have *e*-productions, the *e-free grammars* [2] which are certainly more convenient for developing translators. However, the situation is not hopeless if *e*-productions are present in the grammar, for it is proved that for any context-free language L there exists some *e*-free context-free grammar G such that $L(G) = L \setminus \{e\}$. Building such grammars is rather easy [2].

Context-free grammars match programming languages best of all. These grammars provide rather full description of syntax of real programming languages. Of great importance for translation is the possibility to derive the same sentence from the initial character in different ways.

The derivation $S \Rightarrow a_1 a_2 \ldots a_n$ for $a_i \in T$ and $i = 1, 2, \ldots, n$ is usually represented in the form of a *tree*. The tree vertices are labelled by the characters of the set $T \cup N \cup \{e\}$. The initial character S is used to mark the root of the tree, and terminal characters, to denote leaves. Label all the inner vertices of the tree by nonterminals of the set N.

Let us examine the grammar $(\{E, F, T\}, \{a, b, *, /, +, -, (,)\}, P, E)$ which describes the sequence of arithmetic operations on variables a and b. The set of rules P includes the following productions:

$$E \rightarrow T \mid E + T \mid E - T$$
$$T \rightarrow F \mid T * F \mid T/F$$
$$F \rightarrow a \mid b \mid (E)$$

Because one and the same string can result from several derivations, the latter are divided into two types: left-hand and right-hand derivations. A derivation scheme of the sentence $x \in L(G)$ is called *left-hand* (*right-hand*) if the next rule is always substituted for the extreme left (right) sentential form. Two derivations of the string $a * (a + b) - b$ are written as follows.

The left-hand derivation:

$$E \Rightarrow E - T \Rightarrow T - T \Rightarrow T * F - T \Rightarrow F * F - T \Rightarrow a * F - T$$
$$\Rightarrow a * (E) - T \Rightarrow a * (E + T) - T \Rightarrow a * (T + T) - T$$
$$\Rightarrow a * (F + T) - T \Rightarrow a * (a + T) - T \Rightarrow a * (a + F) - T$$
$$\Rightarrow a * (a + b) - T \Rightarrow a * (a + b) - F \Rightarrow a * (a + b) - b$$

The right-hand derivation:

$$E \Rightarrow E - T \Rightarrow E - F \Rightarrow E - b \Rightarrow T - b \Rightarrow T * F - b$$
$$\Rightarrow T * (E) - b \Rightarrow T * (E + T) - b \Rightarrow T * (E + F) - b$$
$$\Rightarrow T * (E + b) - b \Rightarrow T * (T + b) - b \Rightarrow T * (F + b) - b$$
$$\Rightarrow T * (a + b) - b \Rightarrow F * (a + b) - b \Rightarrow a * (a + b) - b$$

Let us construct a tree for a left-hand derivation of a string (Fig. 1.5). The right-hand derivation tree is the same. Context-free grammar is called *un-*

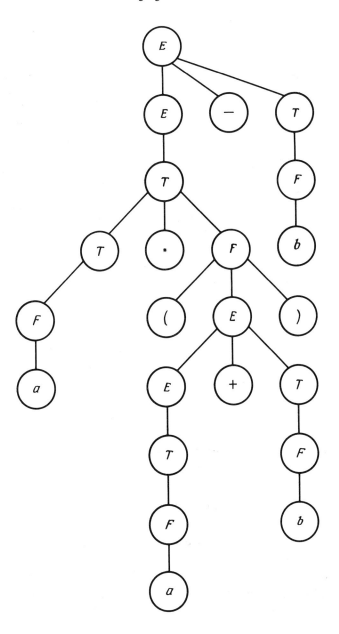

Fig. 1.5. Derivation tree of the string $a * (a + b) - b$

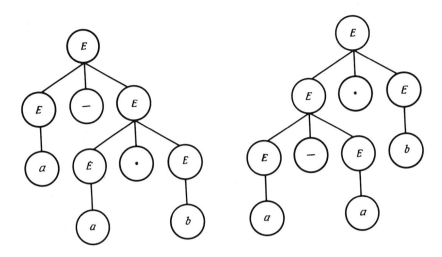

Fig. 1.6. Derivation trees of the expression $a - a * b$

ambiguous, if all possible derivation schemes for the string $x \in L(G)$ correspond to one and the same derivation tree. The grammar $(\{E\}, \{a, +, /, *, -, (,), b\}, P, E)$ exemplifies an *ambiguous grammar*. Its productions are

$$E \rightarrow E + E \mid E - E \mid E * E \mid E/E \mid (E) \mid a \mid b$$

We can construct two different derivation trees for the expression $a - a * b$ (Fig. 1.6). In what follows we shall mainly consider unambiguous grammars.

1.2.3.   Basic Types of Context-Free Grammars

Imposing restrictions on the right-hand parts of productions of context-free grammars (CFG) helps us highlight those enjoying wide practical use. The *s*-grammar is the most simple CFG [5]. The context-free grammar turns into an *s*-grammar subject to the following conditions.

1. The right-hand part of each production should begin with a terminal character.

2. Two productions having identical left-hand parts require that their right-hand parts should begin with different terminal characters.

The grammar $(\{S, T\}, \{a, b\}, P, S)$ exemplifies the *s*-grammar, where the set P contains the productions

$$S \to ab \mid bTT$$
$$T \to b$$

Let us consider one more grammar, $(\{S, A\}, \{a, b, c\}, P, S)$ [5], where P contains

$$S \to aAS \mid b$$
$$A \to cAS \mid e$$

This is not an s-grammar because of the presence of production $A \to e$.

To determine the next type of a more complex context-free grammar, it is necessary to specify the two sets: the set of terminals which *follow* the given nonterminal and the *set of selected productions*. Assign $FL(A)$ for $A \in N$ to the former set, and $CH(p)$, where p is a production $p \in P$, to the latter. Let us define $FL(A)$ for the context-free grammar with the initial S as a set of terminals, which succeed the non-terminal A in some sentential form derived from S. Thus $FL(A) = T'$, if $T' \subset T$ and for every terminal $a \in T'$ the derivation $S \Rightarrow xAay$ exists such that $x,\ y \in (T \cup N)^*$. For instance, $FL(A) = \{a, b\}$ for the grammar given above.

If $A \to ax$ is a grammar production, were $a \in T$ and $x \in (T \cup N)^*$, then $CH(A \to ax) = \{a\}$. If the production has the form $A \to e$, then $CH(A \to e) = FL(A)$. Now we can determine the type of the grammar given above.

Context-free grammar is called *q-grammar* if the following two conditions are fulfilled.

1. The right-hand part of each production either begins with a terminal or is a e-string.

2. The sets of selected productions with identical left-hand parts do not intersect.

In the examined simple CF grammars, the right-hand parts of productions were strings, either empty or beginning with a terminal. Let us remove these restrictions and consider the grammars where the right-hand parts of productions begin both with terminals and nonterminals. Therefore, extend the concept of the set of selected productions and call it the set of directive characters and denote it by $DR(p)$, where $p \in P$.

The set $DR(A \to x) = \{a \mid (x \Rightarrow ay, a \in T \text{ and } y \in (T \cup N)^*)$ or $(x \Rightarrow e$ and $a \in FL(A))\}$. Now we can define the next grammar. A context-free grammar is called the *LL (1) grammar* if the sets of directive characters for the rules with identical left-hand parts do not intersect. Consider ($\{S, F, E, A, B\}$, $\{a, +, *\}$, P, S) as an example of the LL (1) grammar with productions

$$S \to AE$$
$$E \to +AE \mid e$$
$$A \to FB$$
$$B \to *FB \mid e$$
$$F \to a \mid (S)$$

This is a particular case of the LL (k) grammar for $k = 1$. Let us define the LL (k) grammar by introducing the function FIRST.

$$\text{FIRST}_k : T^* \to T^*, \text{ where}$$
$$\text{FIRST}_k (x) = x \text{ if } \mid x \mid \leqslant k$$
$$\text{FIRST}_k (x) = y \text{ if } x = yz, \ y \in T^k, \ z \in T^*$$

Thus, the context-free grammar $G = (N, T, P, S)$ is called the LL (k) *grammar* for some fixed k if there are two left-hand derivations, such that

$$S \overset{*}{\Rightarrow} wAv \Rightarrow wzv \overset{*}{\Rightarrow} wx$$
$$S \overset{*}{\Rightarrow} wAv \Rightarrow wtv \overset{*}{\Rightarrow} wy$$

for which $\text{FIRST}_k (x) = \text{FIRST}_k (y)$ and therefore $z = t$ [1]. Consider an example of the LL (2) grammar with the productions

$$S \to dAS \mid AbSc \mid e$$
$$A \to cbA \mid d$$

Of importance is the fact that LL (k) grammars are unambiguous [2]. Thus, if it is possible to show that the grammar examined is an LL (k) grammar, then it is obviously unambiguous. The above mentioned definitions of LL (k) grammars follow from the left-hand derivation. However a broader scope of languages is determined by the so-called LR-grammars supported by the right-hand derivation.

A context-free grammar $G = (N, T, R, S)$ is referred to as the LR (0) grammar if from the conditions,

(1) none of the productions contains the initial character in its right-hand part;

(2) there are two right-hand schemes of derivation

$$S \overset{*}{\Rightarrow} wAxy \Rightarrow wzxy$$
$$S \overset{*}{\Rightarrow} vBy \Rightarrow vz'y \Rightarrow wzxy$$

where $w, v, z, z' \in (N \cup T)^*$, $A, B \in N$, $x, y \in T^*$, it follows that $A = B$, $z = z'$, $x = e$ [2].

Let us introduce the set LRCONTEXT $(A \to z) = \{v \mid v = wz \in (N \cup T)^*$, where $S \overset{*}{\Rightarrow} wAx \Rightarrow wzx$ is a right-hand scheme of derivation, $x \in T^*$, $w \in (N \cup T)^*\}$. Using this set, it can be shown that the context-free grammar is an $LR(0)$ grammar if

(a) none of its productions contains the initial character in its right-hand part; and

(b) from $v \in$ LRCONTEXT $(A \to z)$ and $vx \in$ LRCONTEXT $(B \to z')$, where $\{A \to z, B \to z'\} \in P$, $z \in (N \cup T)^*$ and $x \in T^*$, it follows that $x = e$, $A = B$, $z = z'$.

Going from the particular to the general we have approached the $LR(k)$ grammars. Proceeding from $G = (N, T, P, S)$, we introduce the complemented grammar $G' = (N', T, P', S')$, where $G' = (N \cup \{S\}, T, P \cup \{S' \to S\}, S')$. Then we call the grammar G an $LR(k)$ *grammar* for $k > 0$ if $vAy = tBx$ (i.e. $v = t$, $A = B$, $x = y$) results from the following conditions:

$$S' \overset{*}{\Rightarrow} vAw \Rightarrow vzw$$
$$S' \overset{*}{\Rightarrow} tBx \Rightarrow vzy$$
$$\text{FIRST}_k(w) = \text{FIRST}_k(y)$$

The grammar presented below exemplifies the $LR(2)$ grammar. Its productions are [6]:

$$S \to F, \ S \mid F$$
$$F \to aL$$
$$L \to b \mid b, \ L$$

Note that the $LR(k)$ grammar generates the $LR(k)$ language which can be either $LR(1)$ language or even $LR(0)$ language under the condition that some termination sign succeeds each sentence.

1.3.   Techniques of Parsing Formal Languages

The previous section dealt with specifying languages by means of formal grammars. Now we are going to discuss the method based on using identifiers. An identifier can be represented in the form of an algorithm determining some set of sentences of the language.

The identifier is comprised of three components (Fig. 1.7): the input tape, the control unit with finite memory, and the auxiliary or working memory [1]. Potentially unlimited on both sides, the *input tape* presents series of cells, each containing the only character of some alphabet T. The extreme left and right cells can be labelled by end-of-the-tape markers.

The reading head indicates a cell of the input tape each time instant. The right (left) shift of the reading head by one cell along the tape corresponds to one step of identification. Note that the head does not transform the current character while reading. Hereinafter, we shall discuss mainly the identifiers where the reading head shifts only from left to right.

The auxiliary memory is intended to store the additional information directly affecting the identification process. Its structure is usually complicated and contains characters of some alphabet M. In particular, the memory can be represented by some structure which consists of strings from the set $L \subset M^*$. Let us introduce two functions. The memory access function is a relation $f : L^* \to M^*$. The function f sets up a correspondence between the current memory state, i.e. the string structure from L^*, and the element of

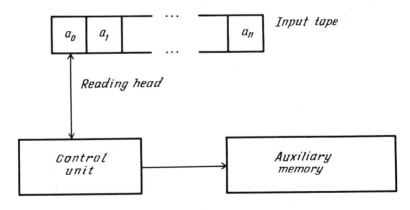

Fig. 1.7. Identifier

the structure, i.e. the string from M^*. The memory transformation function takes the form $h : L^* \times M^* \to M^*$. It transforms the structure of memory in accordance with the information stored, that is the string from M^*. In what follows we shall consider the identifiers with the auxiliary memory realized as stack.

The control unit contains some finite set of states (denoted by Q) which includes the initial state and the subset of finite states. The control unit drives the identifier from one configuration to another. The *configuration* is represented by the triplet (q, x, l), where $q \in Q$ is a current state of the control unit; $x \in M^*$ is the unused part of the input tape with a current character $a \in M$ ($x = ay$, $y \in M^*$) indicated by the reading head; and $l \in L^*$ is the current content of the auxiliary memory.

The starting configuration implies that the control unit is in its initial state, the reading head indicates the leftmost string character of the input tape, and the auxiliary memory contains the initial content. Under *final configuration* the control unit runs into one of its finite states, the reading head indicates the cell following the last string character of the input tape, and the auxiliary storage acquires some predetermined structure.

The step being performed drives the identifier from one configuration to another. Each step is characterized by one and the same sequence of operations:

— the reading head shifts one cell to the right;

— the memory content modifies depending on both the character read from the input tape and the memory state;

— the state of the control unit changes according to the current state of the input tape and the control unit and as well as to the content of the auxiliary memory.

If each step of identification admits no more than one configuration for the identifier to pass to, we deal with a *deterministic identifier*. Several configurations admitted are inherent in an *indeterministic identifier*. The identifier is said *to admit a string* if having placed it onto the input tape, it goes over into one of final configurations from the initial one. A set of strings admitted constitutes a *language determined by the identifier*.

While operating the identifier establishes the syntactic structure of a sentence according to the parsing tree. The process of constructing a tree for parsing the source sentence is called *parsing* or *syntactic analysis*. Having numbered the grammar productions, we can represent the analysis of a real sentence by series of numbers of the productions used while deriving this sen-

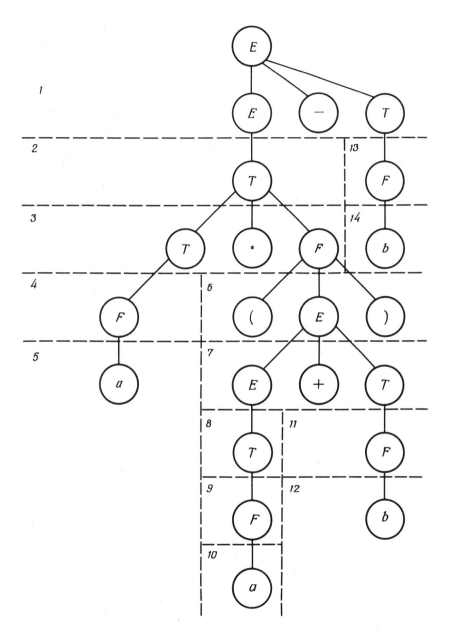

Fig. 1.8. Top-down constructed tree

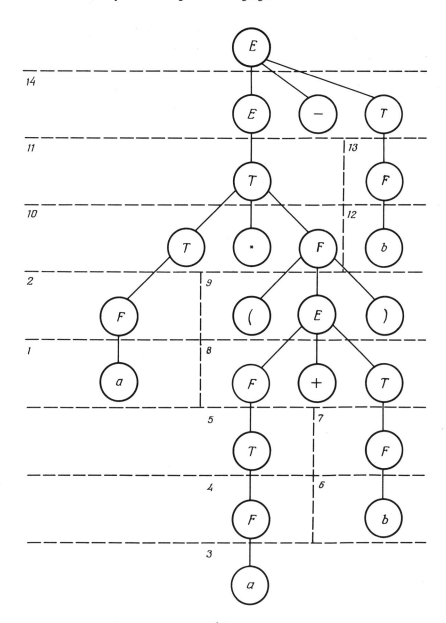

Fig. 1.9. Bottom-up constructed tree

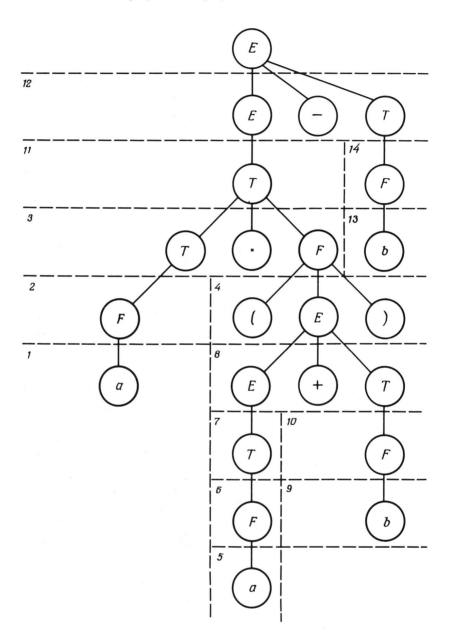

Fig. 1.10. Horizontal parsing version

tence. Let us number the grammar rules given in Sec. 1.2.2:

$$E \rightarrow E + E \tag{1}$$
$$E \rightarrow E - E \tag{2}$$
$$E \rightarrow E * E \tag{3}$$
$$E \rightarrow E/E \tag{4}$$
$$E \rightarrow (E) \tag{5}$$
$$E \rightarrow a \tag{6}$$
$$E \rightarrow b \tag{7}$$

Thus parsing the string $a - a * b$ corresponds to one of two sequences, either 2, 6, 3, 6, 7 or 3, 2, 6, 6, 7 (Fig. 1.6). *Left parsing* of the string x implies the set of productions involved in left-hand derivation of the string x from the initial character S. The above example shows two variants of left parsing. *Right parsing* of the string x represents the inverted sequence of productions involved in right-hand derivation of the string x from the initial character S. The sequence {6, 6, 7, 3, 2} illustrates right parsing of the string $a - a * b$.

Parsing techniques can be generally represented by two principal methods — top-down and bottom-up. The *top-down (descending)* building of a tree begins with its root. Each inner node develops if all the parent nodes are known and constructed. We select the production for developing the inner node basing on the current characters of both the input tape and the auxiliary memory. Figure 1.8 illustrates the top-down construction of a tree shown in Fig. 1.5.

The *bottom-up* construction of a tree begins with its leaves. Each next node of the tree should be built if all the sibling nodes belong to the part of the tree, which has been already constructed. Figure 1.9 shows the tree of Fig. 1.5 constructed bottom-up. This parsing technique is also called *ascending*. Recently, a number of methods have appeared which directly do not use any of the two parsing techniques suggested here. *Horizontal parsing*, for example, takes account of a node either dangling and corresponding to some current character of the input tape or preceding the examined node [7]. Figure 1.10 illustrates a tree which matches horizontal parsing.

1.3.1.   Finite Automatons

A finite automaton is a quintuple

$$A = (Q, \; T, \; t, \; q_0, \; F)$$

where Q = finite set of automaton states

T = nonempty finite set of input characters, i.e. input alphabet

$q_0 \in Q$ = *initial state*

$F \subseteq Q$ = nonempty set of automaton final states

t = transition function

$$t : Q \times T^* \rightarrow R(Q)$$

Such an automaton operates as an identifier (Fig. 1.11). The tape contains the input string with two end markers on both sides. The control unit is in its initial state q_0. The input tape is examined character-by-character from left to right. Suppose that the characters $a_0 a_1 \ldots a_{i-1}$ are examined by the reading head and the control unit is in the q_{i-1} state. The character a_i is considered admissible if there is at least one state $t(q_{i-1}, a_i) \in Q$. In the absence of such a state, the automaton stops scanning. In the general case, the identifier becomes indeterministic in the presence of several similar states. Hence we shall have to deal with the *indeterministic finite automaton.*

The automaton accepts the string $x = a_1 a_2 \ldots a_n \in T^+$ if some sequence of states $q_0, q_1, \ldots, q_n$ exists such that $q_{i+1} - t(q_i, a_{i+1})$ for $i = 0, 1, \ldots, n - 1$ and $q_n \in F$, and the character a_n which has been read last, is followed by the end marker. The beginning marker is expected to be read in the q_0-state. Using the transition function, this can be expressed as $t(q_0, x) \in F$. Consider the transition function corresponding to one step of identification as a particular case of its general notation for the string x containing only

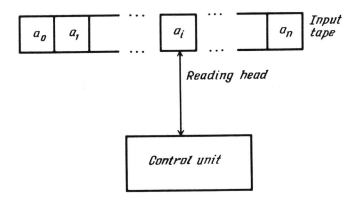

Fig. 1.11. Identifier — finite-state automaton

one character $x = a_{i+1}$ and the q_i-state. Thus, the function t can be recursively presented in the form $t(q, x) = t(t(q, a), y)$ if the string $x = ay$ for $a \in T$ and $y \in T^*$ is valid.

Let us write the set of all the strings $T(A)$ admitted by the automaton A as

$$T(A) = \{x \mid x \in T^* \text{ and } t(q_0, x) \in F\}$$

If $G = (N, T, P, S)$ is a right linear grammar, then, as stated in [4], there exists a finite automaton such that $T(A) = L(G)$. This automaton is constructed from the grammar by proceeding as follows. The set of states can be obtained by joining the set of nonterminal characters and the specially introduced finite state $\{f\} = F$. Thus, $Q = N \cup F$. Hence the initial state coincides with the initial grammar character, i.e. $q_0 = S$. The set of terminal characters T constitutes the input alphabet. The transition functions for each grammar production are defined as follows:

$t(B, a) = C$ for the rule $B \to aC \in P$ and $B \in N$, $C \in N$, $a \in T$;

$t(B, a) = \{f\}$ for the rule $B \to a \in P$; and

$t(B, a) = \varnothing$ for all other cases.

Thus, the number of elements from the domain of transition fucntion for which its value is not an empty set, is exactly equal to the number of grammar productions.

Using *transition graphs,* otherwise called *state graphs,* transition functions can be conveniently specified. The state graph (V, E) is oriented and constructed in the following manner. Assign a vertex from the set V to each state of the set Q.

Circles depict all the vertices except for finite ones. The starting vertex corresponding to the initial state is marked with an arrow. A rectangle represents the final vertex. The edge $(B, C) \in E$ belongs to the graph if for some pair of a character and a state, i.e. $a \in T$ and $B \in Q$, the value of function $t(B, a)$ is not empty and is equal to $C \in Q$. Figure 1.12 shows the state graph for the automaton A.

$A = (\{q_0, q_1, q_2, q_3, q_4\}, t, q, \{q_3, q_4,\})$

where $t(q_0, a) = q_1$

$\quad t(q_0, b) = q_2$

$\quad t(q_1, b) = q_4$

$\quad t(q_2, c) = q_3$

$\quad t(q_2, a) = q_4$

$\quad t(q_4, c) = q_3$

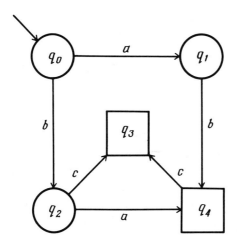

Fig. 1.12. State graph

Figure 1.13 shows the state graph of the automaton proceeding from the right linear grammar $G = (\{B, C, D)\}, \{a, b, c, d\}, P, B)$. Let us reveal the correspondence between the productions of the grammar G and the elements of transition function of the automaton.

$$
\begin{array}{ll}
B \to bC & t\,(B, b) = C \\
B \to d & t\,(B, d) = f \\
C \to cC & t\,(C, c) = C \\
C \to bD & t\,(C, b) = D \\
D \to a & t\,(D, a) = f
\end{array}
$$

where f is the final state of the automaton.

Let us consider another example of grammar generating the sentences

$$a,\ a0,\ a00,\ \ldots,\ b,\ b0,\ b00,\ b000,\ \ldots$$

The grammar productions are

$$S \to a \mid aD \mid bD$$
$$D \to 0 \mid 0D$$

We construct a finite-state automaton for this grammar. Its state graph is

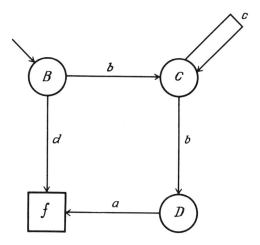

Fig. 1.13. State graph for right linear grammar

shown in Fig. 1.14. It is obvious from the graph that the finite automaton is indeterministic because two edges each loaded with *a* leave the state *S*. The transition function takes on two values for the character *a* in the state *S*:

$$t\,(S,\,a) = \{f\}$$
$$t\,(S,\,a) = D$$

The use of indeterministic automaton for parsing is rather intricate. There-

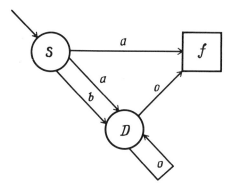

Fig. 1.14. State graph for indeterministic automaton

fore, we are interested in conversion of the automaton from the indeterministic to the deterministic form. The problem can certainly be solved for finite-state automatons. As is shown in [4], a deterministic automaton A' exists for some indeterministic automaton A such that $T(A) = T(A')$. Let the transition function $t(q, a)$ have a set of values $Q' \subset Q$. Consider this set a new state q'. Add this state to the set of automaton states Q, i.e. $Q = Q \cup q'$. Now let us define the transition function for the new state q'.

$$t(q', a) = t(Q', a) = \bigcup_{i \in Q'} t(i, a) \text{ for all } a \in T$$

Having performed the given transformation for all transition functions taking on more than one value, we will receive the deterministic automaton. Let us write down all transition functions for the above example.

$$t(S, a) = \{f\}$$
$$t(S, a) = D$$
$$t(S, b) = D$$
$$t(D, 0) = D$$
$$t(D, 0) = \{f\}$$

Introduce the new state $q' = \{D, f\}$ and rewrite the transition functions

$$t(S, a) = q'$$
$$t(S, b) = D$$

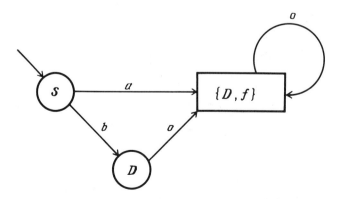

Fig. 1.15. State graph for deterministic finite-state automaton

$t(D, 0) = q'$

$t(q', 0) = q'$ since f is a finite state from $\{D, f\}$ and $t(D, 0) = q'$

Figure 1.15 shows the state graph of the obtained deterministic automaton.

1.3.2.   Push-Down Automatons

Finite-state automatons enable constructing the identifier for the language generated by the right linear grammar. The next type of automatons is intended to identify context-free languages. The more complicated language we study, the more complicated automaton we need. A push-down automaton is a one-way and usually indeterministic identifier using stack for auxiliary memory (Fig. 1.16). The stack can be represented by the character string. The rightmost character is the *bottom of the stack* and the leftmost one is its *top*. At a certain instant of time only the top character of the stack can be read out of the string. The character, once read-out, is deleted and the next (right) character becomes the top. On recording the characters, they move to the left from the top. The last character is considered as a new top of the stack.

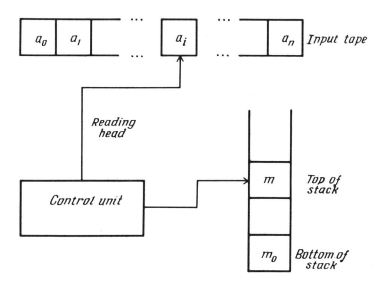

Fig. 1.16. Identifier — push-down automaton

The push-down automaton is represented by the following septet

$$A = (Q, T, M, t, q_0, m_0, F)$$

where Q = finite set of states

T = finite input alphabet

M = infinite alphabet of stack characters (stack alphabet)

$q_0 \in Q$ = initial state of automaton

$m_0 \in M$ = initial stack character

$F \subseteq Q$ = nonempty set of final states

t = transition function

$$t : Q \times (T \cup \{e\})/M \to R\,(Q \times M^*)$$

The automaton associates the set of all the subsets $Q \times M^*$ with the triplets, which consist of a state, some current input character of the input tape or an empty character e and a top of the stack. Before the processing starts, the input tape contains the source sentence limited by markers on both sides. The reading head indicates the first character of the sentence. The stack is empty and keeps the initial stack character. The push-down automaton is in its initial state. In the process of functioning, the input tape is examined from left to right, without any resettings. The automaton converts from one configuration to another in each step.

The configuration of a push-down automaton is defined by the triplet (q, x, v), where $v \in M^*$ is the stack content; $q \in Q$ is the current state of the push-down automaton; and $x \in T^*$ is a segment of the source string of the input tape, which begins with some current character indicated by the reading head and ends with the last character of the string.

The configuration can also be represented in the form of (q, x, vm_0) or (q, x, mv) or (q, x, mvm_0), where $m \in M$ is the top character of the stack. Therefore the starting configuration should be specified as (q_0, x, m_0) and the final configuration as (q, e, v) for $q \in F$ and $v \in M^*$. To record the conversion of the automaton from one configuration to another, use will be made of binary relation $\vdash$ defined on automaton configurations. For a pair of $(q', b) \in t\,(q, a, m)$ and $q', q \in Q$ let us write

$$(q, ay, mv) \vdash (q', y, bv)$$

where $a \in T \cup \{e\}$, $y \in T^*$, $m \in M$, $v, b \in M^*$. Consider the character $a \neq e$ admissible if the automaton having read it out of the input string goes over from the configuration (q, ay, mv) to (q', y, bv). The reading head shifts to the right by one character and the string b of stack characters replaces the top character m. For $b = e$ the stack content reduces by the character m and the next stack character becomes its top.

The push-down automaton admits some character string $x = a_1, a_2, \ldots,$ $a_i, \ldots, a_n \in T^*$, where $a_i \in T \cup \{e\}$, $i = 1, 2, \ldots, n$, for a sequence of configurations, such that

$$(q_{i-1}, a_i, \ldots, a_n, v_{i-1}) \vdash (q_i, a_{i+1}, \ldots, a_n, v_i)$$

where $q_0, q_1, \ldots, q_n \in Q$, $v_0, v_1, \ldots, v_n \in M^*$, $q_n \in F$, $a_n = e$.

Because the space characters are of little interest for compiler designers, let us delete them from the definition of the string to be admitted. Thus, the automaton A admits the string $a_1 a_2 \ldots a_n \in T^*$ for $a_i \in T$ and $i = 1, 2, \ldots,$ n if there exists an identical admissible string where $a_i \in T \cup \{e\}$. The series of configurations accepted by the push-down automaton, while identifying the string x, should be expressed as

$$(q_0, x, m_0) \vdash {}^*(q_n, e, v_n)$$

for $q_n \in F$, $v_n \in M^*$. If the final and initial $(v_n = m_0)$ states of the stack are identical, the string $x \in T^*$ is said to be admissible for the automaton A with the *exhausted stack* [4]

$$(q_0, x, m_0) \vdash {}^* (q_n, e, m_0)$$

If the stack of the automaton contains the initial character, which is a space character, $m_0 = e$, then the automaton is considered to admit the string x with *empty stack*.

$$(q_0, x, e) \vdash {}^* (q_n, e, e)$$

A set of strings defined below constitutes the language $T(A)$ acceptable for the push-down automaton:

$$T(A) = \{x \mid x \in T^* \text{ and } (q_0, x, m_0) \vdash {}^* (q, e, v), q \in F, v \in M^*\}$$

Each step of the automaton permits the top character to be either deleted or replaced with a string of finite length containing stack characters. Let us lift this restriction to specify the extended push-down automaton [1], which enables finite-length strings adjacent to the stack top to be substituted. The given automaton is indeterministic because $t(q, a, v)$ and $t(q, e, v)$ have a set of values (the set can have even more than one element) and there is no general rule for selecting the unique value out of the set. If the set is empty, the automaton cannot accept the next input characters.

The considered push-down automatons can operate as indeterministic identifiers of context-free languages. As is shown in [1, 4], each context-free grammar $G = (N, T, P, S)$ matches the push-down automaton A such that $T(A) = L(G)$. Let us construct some push-down automaton in the form of top-down identifier. To this end, we determine the sets specifying the automaton A:

$$Q = \{q\} \qquad = \text{the set of states}$$
$$T \qquad\qquad = \text{input alphabet comprising terminals}$$
$$M = N \cup T = \text{stack alphabet of terminals and nonterminals}$$
$$q_0 = q \qquad = \text{initial state}$$
$$m_0 = S \qquad = \text{initial stack character}$$
$$F = \varnothing \qquad = \text{set of finite empty states}$$

The transition function t is defined as follows:

— if the set of productions P contains the rule $A \rightarrow v$, then $t(q, e, A)$ contains (q, v) for all the productions having the nonterminal A in their left-hand parts

— $t(q, a, a) = \{(q, e)\}$ for all $a \in T$

Now let us construct the push-down automaton for the grammar discussed in Section 1.2.2 with the productions

$$E \rightarrow T \mid E + T \mid E - T$$
$$T \rightarrow F \mid T * F \mid T/F$$
$$F \rightarrow a \mid b \mid (E)$$

The automaton is represented by the septet $(q, T, T \cup N, t, q, E, \varnothing)$. Its transition function is as follows:

$$t(q, e, E) = \{(q, T), (q, E + T), (q, E - T)\}$$
$$t(q, e, T) = \{(q, F), (q, T * F), (q, T/F)\}$$

$$t(q, e, F) = \{(q, a), (q, b), (q, (E))\}$$
$$t(q, d, d) = \{(q, e) \text{ for all } d \in \{a, b, +, -, *, /, (,)\}$$

Figure 1.5 shows the derivation tree of the string $a * (a + b) - b$. Identifying the string, the automaton can pass through the following configurations:

$$(q, a * (a + b) - b, E) \vdash (q, a * (a + b) - b, E - T)$$
$$\vdash (q, a * (a + b) - b, T - T)$$
$$\vdash (q, a * (a + b) - b, T * F - T)$$
$$\vdash (q, a * (a + b) - b, F * F - T)$$
$$\vdash (q, a * (a + b) - b, a * F - T)$$
$$\vdash (q, * (a + b) - b, * F - T)$$
$$\vdash (q, (a + b) - b, F - T)$$
$$\vdash (q, (a + b) - b, (E) - T)$$
$$\vdash (q, a + b) - b, (E) - T)$$
$$\vdash (q, a + b) - b, E + T) - T)$$
$$\vdash (q, a + b) - b, T + T) - T)$$
$$\vdash (q, a + b) - b, F + T) - T)$$
$$\vdash (q, a + b) - b, a + T) - T)$$
$$\vdash (q, + b) - b, +T) - T)$$
$$\vdash (q, b) - b, T) - T)$$
$$\vdash (q, b) - b, F) - T)$$
$$\vdash (q, b) - b, b) - T)$$
$$\vdash (q,) - b,) - T)$$
$$\vdash (q, -b, -T)$$
$$\vdash (q, b, T)$$
$$\vdash (q, b, F)$$
$$\vdash (q, b, b)$$
$$\vdash (q, e, e)$$

Let us represent in the form of a graph (V, E') the indeterministic automaton simulating left-hand derivations of strings. Construct the set V to associate each vertex with some nonterminal character. Complement the set with a special (terminal) vertex to admit the input characters of the string and denote it by g. Then $V' = N \cup \{g\}$. The edge (A, B) connects two vertices labelled with nonterminal characters $A, B \in N$, if the value of transition function $t(q, e, A) = \{(q, v)\}$ is not empty and $v = Bw \in M^+$, $w' \in M^*$, $w \in M^*$. On passing along such an edge of the graph the automaton executes the step $(q, x, Aw') \vdash (q, x, Bww')$, where $x \in T^*$. If $v = e$, complement the graph with the edge (A, g) for the automaton to execute the step $(q, x, Aw') \vdash (q, x, w')$. For $v = aw$ the edge (A, g) being introduced provides the step $(q, x, Aw') \vdash (q, x, aww')$. For the values of $t(q, a, a) = (q, e)$, where $a \in T$, the edge (g, g) is introduced, which matches the step $(q, ax, aw) \vdash (q, x, w)$. Now we have all the nodes of the graph connected in accordance with the transition function. However, no edges rise from the node g. Let us link the vertex g with all the others without complementing the transition function. The transition along such an edge does not change the automaton configuration. Thus the step $(q, x, Aw) \vdash (q, x, Aw)$ matches the edge (g, A). The change of configurations caused by passing an edge is determined by the triplet

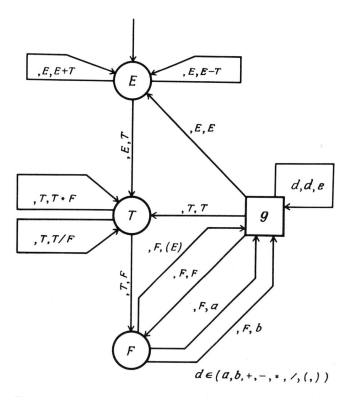

Fig. 1.17. State graph for indeterministic push-down automaton

(a, b, c), where a is an admissible character of the input tape, b is either a character or a character string (for the extended automaton) to be deleted from the stack, and c is a character string to be put into stack. Let us mark the edges to match the following steps:

$$
\begin{array}{llll}
(q, x, Aw') \vdash (q, x, Bww') & e, A, Bw & \text{or} & , A, Bw \\
(q, x, Aw') \vdash (q, x, w') & e, A, e & & , A, e \\
(q, x, Aw') \vdash (q, x, aww') & e, A, aw & & , A, aw \\
(q, ax, aw) \vdash (q, x, w) & a, a, e & & \\
(q, x, Aw) \vdash (q, x, Aw) & e, A, A & & , A, A
\end{array}
$$

The state graph for the push-down automaton is shown in Fig. 1.17. As already mentioned, an *extended push-down automaton* simulating the right-hand derivation of the string $a * (a + b) - b$ can be constructed as follows [1]:

$$
\begin{aligned}
Q &= \{q, r\} = \text{set of states} \\
T &= \text{input alphabet} \\
M &= N \cup T \cup \{\#\} = \text{alphabet of stack characters} \\
q &= \text{initial state of the automaton} \\
\# &= \text{initial stack character} \\
\{r\} &= \text{set of final states}
\end{aligned}
$$

The transition function

$$
\begin{aligned}
&t(q, e, v) \text{ contains } (q, A) \text{ if } A \to v \text{ is a grammar production} \\
&t(q, a, e) = \{(q, a)\} \text{ for all } a \in T \\
&t(q, e, \#S) = \{(r, e)\}
\end{aligned}
$$

To specify the automaton, we have to define the graph (V', E') with a set of nodes $\{r, q\} \cup N$. Assign the edge (B, A) of the graph to the function $(q, A) \in t(q, e, v)$ for $v = zB \in M^+$ such that the transition along this edge would match the step $(q, e, \#wzB) \vdash (q, e, \#wA)$ for $w \in M^*$. In what follows, configurations of automatons will be recorded in the form of the inverted stack string, i.e. the stack bottom will be the leftmost character of the string and its top — the rightmost one. If $v = e$, then set the edge (g, A) for the automaton step $(q, e, \#w) \vdash (q, e, \#wA)$. Analogously, if $v = zd$, $d \in T$, $z \in M^*$. Set the edge (g, A) corresponding to the step

$(q, e \# wv) \vdash (q, e \# wA)$. The edge (g, g) associates with character transfer from the input tape to the stack with the step $(q, ax, \#w) \vdash (q, x, \#wa)$ in accordance with the function $t (q, a, e) = \{(q, a)\}$. To admit the initial character of the grammar S, the edge (S, r) matching the step $(q, e, \#S) \vdash (r, e, e)$ for the function $t (q, e, \#S) = \{(r, e)\}$. After each substitution of a nonterminal by the stack substring it is possible to transfer characters from the input tape to the stack by introducing the edges (A, g) which will not affect the automaton configuration.

Let us construct the automaton for the grammar examined above. It is represented by the septet $(\{q, r\}, T, M, t, q, \#, \{r\})$. The automaton transition function is as follows:

$$
\begin{aligned}
t (q, e, E + T) \quad &= \{(q, E)\} \\
t (q, e, E - T) \quad &= \{(q, E)\} \\
t (q, e, T) \quad &= \{(q, E\} \\
t (q, e, T * F) \quad &= \{(q, T\} \\
t (q, e, T/F) \quad &= \{(q, T)\} \\
t (q, e, F) \quad &= \{(q, T)\} \\
t (q, e, a) \quad &= \{(q, F)\} \\
t (q, e, b) \quad &= \{(q, F)\} \\
t (q, e, (E)) \quad &= \{(q, F)\} \\
t (q, d, e) \quad &= \{(q, d)\} \text{ for all } d \in \{a, b, +, /, -, *, (,)\} \\
t (q, e, \#E) \quad &= \{(r, e)\}
\end{aligned}
$$

Figure 1.18 shows the state graph of the given automaton. The automaton identifies the string $a * (a + b) - b$ in the following order:

$$
\begin{aligned}
(q, a * (a + b) - b, \#) &\vdash (q, * (a + b), - b, \#a) \\
&\vdash (q, * (a + b) - b, \#F) \\
&\vdash (q, * (a + b) - b, \#T) \\
&\vdash (q, (a + b) - b, \#T *) \\
&\vdash (q, a + b) - b, \#T * ( ) \\
&\vdash (q, +b) - b, \#T * (a) \\
&\vdash (q, +b) - b, \#T * (F) \\
&\vdash (q, +b) - b, \#T * (T) \\
&\vdash (q, +b) - b, \#T * (E)
\end{aligned}
$$

$$\vdash (q, b) - b, \#T * (E +)$$
$$\vdash (q,) - b, \#T * (E + b)$$
$$\vdash (q,) - b, \#T * (E + F)$$
$$\vdash (q,) - b, \#T * (E + T)$$
$$\vdash (q,) - b, \#T * (E)$$
$$\vdash (q, -b, \#T * (E))$$
$$\vdash (q, -b, \#T * F)$$
$$\vdash (q, -b, \#T)$$
$$\vdash (q, -b, \#E)$$
$$\vdash (q, b, \#E -)$$
$$\vdash (q, e, \#E - b)$$
$$\vdash (q, e, \#E - F)$$
$$\vdash (q, e, \#E - T)$$
$$\vdash (q, e, \#E)$$
$$\vdash (r, e, e)$$

Both versions of the push-down automatons observed, perfectly correspond with context-free grammars. Nevertheless, they are ineffective in translator design for recursive languages (e.g. Pascal, Ada, etc.) since they are indeterministic. Indeterministic parsing presumes resets and recursive languages demand resets in parsing both the current string and the whole program. During translation parsing concurs with semantic operations to be performed on the program. The reset may cause cancellation of the operations executed. This impedes processing and sometimes makes resetting impossible.

The possibility of constructing an automaton as well as its determinacy depend on the type of context-free grammar. Theory highlights $LL(k)$ and $LR(k)$ grammars which permits of constructing deterministic push-down automatons using top-down and bottom-up techniques. Earlier, we have discussed the restrictions imposed on these context-free grammars. The well-known methods of creating deterministic automatons for $LL(k)$ and $LR(k)$ grammars are discussed in detail in [1, 6, 7], therefore, we will not dwell on them here. Nevertheless, our book aims at careful study of these problems basing on the new approach suggested here.

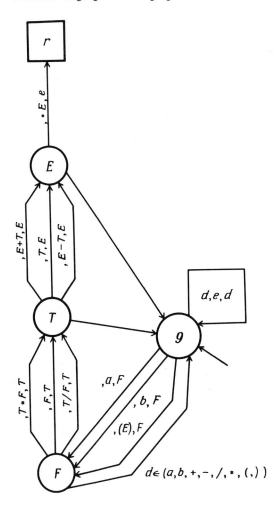

Fig. 1.18. State graph for extended push-down automaton

1.4.   Syntax and Semantics of Languages

As already mentioned, by semantics is meant the rules of imposing a meaning to syntax constructs. Though the means specifying syntax of formal grammars are sufficiently developed, the translator designers lack analogous techniques for semantics. Therefore, the semantics of a language is usually described in words. Nevertheless, some methods provide its rigorous definition. One such method is based on the use of attribute grammars. The language syntax is described by context-free grammars and the semantics, by a number of attributes with a set of semantic functions that permit one to determine some attributes from others.

The attribute grammar G [7] consists of the following components. The context-free grammar $G = (N, T, P, S)$ is the basis. The mappings $J: (N \cup T) \to A_J'$ and $S: (N \cup T) \to A_S'$ associate each character $x \in (N \cup T)$ with disjoint sets of attributes both inherited $(A_J \subset A_J')$ and synthesized $(A_S \subset A_S')$, i.e. $A_J \cap A_S = \varnothing$. The set of rules $F(p)$ intended to determine the attribute meanings is the last component. Let $p = X_0 \to x_1 x_2 \ldots x_n$ be a rule from the set P. Then the character x_j of the rule p is said to have the attribute $(a_{p,j})$ if $a \in A(x_j) = J(x_j) \cup S(x_j)$. Let $A_P = \bigcup\limits_{j=0}^{n} a_{p,j}$ be a set of attributes synthesized, attached to x_0, (if they do exist and there is no attribute $a_{p,j} = \varnothing$) and of those inherited, attached to x_j for $j > 0$. Then $F(p)$ consists of $k = |A_p| < n$ rules for determining the elements $a \in A_p$, each rule of the form $a := f(a_1, \ldots, a_t)$. The attributes $a_1, \ldots, a_t$ of the rule p differ from a and the semantic function f enables one to evaluate a by the values of $a_1, \ldots, a_t$. The function is usually recorded in some programming language.

The attribute tree is a good illustration to interrelationship of syntax and semantics. This is a derivation tree expressed in context-free grammars, whose nodes bear appropriate attributes. The evaluation of attributes complies with certain rules. The attributes being synthesized ignore the parent-sibling relations. Thus there are involved attributes which belong to the subtree with a root represented by the node bearing the given attribute synthesized. On the other hand, evaluating the inherited attributes takes no account of those belonging to the nodes of the subtree.

The global and structured attributes should also be highlighted in addition to those already mentioned. To this end, use can be made of global attributes at any point of their scope. In particular, this may be the whole subtree whose root belongs to the global attribute. If this subtree, in its turn, contains a subtree with the same name as the attribute, the latter subtree is excluded from the scope of the global attribute. Structured attributes are analogous to structured variables applied in programming languages. Consider an example of the attribute grammar [7].

The program P represents the block B. Each block contains the data block LD and the list of instructions LS separated by semicolon and parenthesized. The instruction can be either a block or an identifier I. The latter should be described in the block which includes the instruction. The routine should not include undeclared instructions. The attribute grammar is represented below.

$E \rightarrow b$

　　E.environment : $= \varnothing$

　　E.error : $=$ B.error

$B \rightarrow$ (LD; LS)

　　B. environment : $=$ environment $\cup$ LD.list

　　B.error : $=$ LS.error

LD $\rightarrow$ I

　　LD.list : $=$ I.name

$LD_1 \rightarrow LD_2$, I

　　LD_1.list : $= LD_2$.list $\cup$ I.name

LS $\rightarrow$ S

　　LS.error : $=$ S.error

$LS_1 \rightarrow LS_2$, S

　　LS_1.error : $= LS_2$.error $\vee$ S.error

S $\rightarrow$ I

　　S.error : $=$ I.name $\notin$ environment

S $\rightarrow$ B

　　S.error : $=$ B.error

In the grammar the record $X.a$ denotes the attribute a attached to the character X. If the character X is not shown, the attribute is attached to the last character coupled with the attribute. The attributes, environment, error, list and name, are assigned to grammar characters as follows:

$A\,(E) = A\,(B) = \{$environment, error$\}$

$A\,(LD) = \{$list$\}$

$A\,(S) = A\,(LS) = \{$error$\}$

$A\,(I) = \{$name$\}$

The interrelationship of language syntax and semantics will be described in terms of attributes as well. However, this approach makes the names of attributes to correspond only to nonterminal characters independent of their location in the rule.

So, we have discussed the basic methods of specifying syntax and semantics. Both syntax and semantics of every language associate with its inherent real or *meant language processor* which defines the language unambiguously [8]. Various translators and compilers may be considered as realizations of language processors.

2 Analysis of Context-Free Language Processors

Creating language processors is a time-consuming job. Therefore, it is desired that the original problem statement should be simple and permit of complete description of language syntax and semantics. An oriented loaded graph is taken as basic representation of a language processor. A similar graph is applied in R-technology [9]. Each edge of the graph (v_1, v_2) has a certain load (Fig. 2.1).

A predicate P or some condition concerning the transition along the given edge should be superscribed above the edge. Both terminal and nonterminal characters, contexts and dummy predicates are considered as predicates. An operation F, which matches the transition along the given edge, should be subscribed under the edge. The performed operations are recorded in programming languages.

A number of graph transformations and a transition instruction for the graphs already reduced will help proceed to a language processor from the problem statement. The techniques suggested can be computerized. The method is based on reducing the state graph to its deterministic form for the system of finite automatons, which corresponds to context-free grammars. Taking account of the contexts we will redefine the transition instruction for context-sensitive languages.

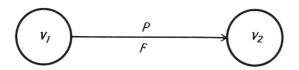

Fig. 2.1. Processor representation

2.1. Processor Representation

Let us examine a context-free formal grammar represented by the quadruple $G = (N, T, P, N_1)$, where N is a set of nonterminal characters; T is a set of terminal characters; P is a set of productions $v \to w$ for $v \in N$, $w \in (T \cup N)^+$; N_1 is an initial character, $N_1 \in N$. This grammar associates with a system of finite automatons [4] such that

$$T(A) = L(G)$$

where

$$T(A) = \bigcup_{z \in T(A_1)} \{x \in T^* \mid z \overset{*}{\underset{A}{\Rightarrow}} x\}$$

is a language admitted by the system of automatons A;

$$L(G) = \{x \in T^* \mid N_1 \overset{*}{\underset{G}{\Rightarrow}} x\}$$

is a language generated by the grammar G; z is a sentence of the language admitted by the automaton A_1; A_1 is an initial automaton of the system A. Let us denote the finite automaton by A_i and the corresponding nonterminal character by N_i to provide the uniformity for notation.

The system of finite automatons constitutes the nonempty set $\{A_1, A_2, \ldots, A_n\}$. Here A_1 is the initial automaton and each A_i is specified by the quintuple $(Q_i, T_i \cup Q', t_i, q_{0i}, F_i)$, where T_i is a set of input characters (terminals), Q_i is a nonempty finite set of states, $q_{0i} \in Q_i$ is an initial state, $F_i \in Q_i$ is a final state, t_i is a transition function

$$t_i : Q_i \times (T_i \cup Q') \to R(Q_i)$$

Here

$$Q' = \bigcup_{i=1}^{n} \{\text{lab}(q_{0i})\}$$

lab (y) is a labelling function

$$\text{lab}(y) = (y = e \to e, y - T \to y, y = q_{0i} \to {}'q_{0i}')$$

which sets up a correspondence between each state and the label of the initial state. If Q_i and Q_k are the sets of states of automatons A_i and A_k $(i \neq k)$, i.e.

$Q_i \cap Q_k = \emptyset$, then $Q = \bigcup\limits_{i=1}^{n} Q_i$, $T = \bigcup\limits_{i=1}^{n} T_i$. Hence, the transition function of the automaton A_i will take the form

$$t_i : Q \times (T \cup Q') \to R(Q)$$

where $R(Q)$ is a set of all the subsets of the states Q.

Let us define the automaton A_i proceeding from the series of all the productions $P : N_i \to u^i_{j,\,1} u^i_{j,\,2} \ldots$ which contain one and the same nonterminal character $N_i \in N$ in their left-hand parts. This character matches the initial state q_{0i} with a label $'N_i'$. The number of such productions (m_i) varies for different nonterminals. The state graph of such an automaton is shown in Fig. 2.2 where $u^i_{j,\,l} \in N \cup T$, $q_i = \bigcup\limits_{l}^{n_j} \bigcup\limits_{j}^{m} v^i_{j,\,l} \cup 'N_i'$, $j = 1, 2, \ldots, m,\ l = = 1, 2, \ldots, n_j$, $v^i_{j,\,n_j} = F_i$ for all the values of j. Thus, constructing the i-th automaton proceeds from m productions and comprises m routes from the initial state to the final one. Each j-th route contains n_j nodes, where the last node always corresponds to some finite state of automaton.

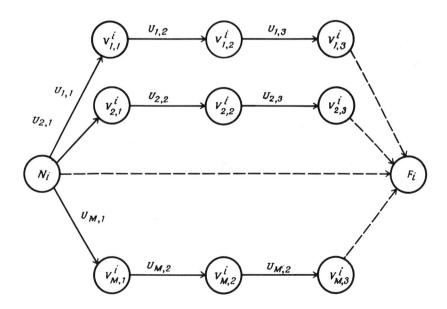

Fig. 2.2. State graph for finite-state automaton A

Let us consider this system of finite-state automatons as a sentence identifier for context-free languages. During the identification process we shall simulate the left-hand derivation of the string being processed. The tape saves the input string. The control unit is in its initial state $'N_1'$. The transition along the edge loaded with a terminal character becomes possible if the current character or the character group is identical to the mentioned terminal. Such a transition implies that the current character of the input tape is admissible. The transition along the edge loaded with a nonterminal character is possible if the automaton goes to its finite state from the initial one, whose label is identical to the loaded nonterminal. The input string is considered admissible if all its characters including the end mark are admitted and the identifier runs into the finite state F_1 of the automaton A_1, which corresponds to the initial grammar character.

Let us extend the definition of the transition function in accordance with (2.1) and the procedure accepted for scanning language sentences:

$$t\,(v^i_{j,\,l}, u^i_{j,\,l+1}) = \{v^i_{j,\,l+1}\}$$
$$t\,('N'_i, u^i_{j,\,l}) = \{v^i_{j,\,l}\} \tag{2.2}$$

for
$$u^i_{j,\,l+1}, u^i_{j,\,l} \in T$$
$$t\,(v^i_{j,\,l},\ u^i_{j,\,l+1}) = \{u^i_{j,\,l+1}\} \tag{2.3}$$

for lab $(N_k) = 'N'_k = u^i_{j,\,l+1} \in Q'$ (at $k = i$ the direct recursive inversion takes place);

$$t\,(F_i, e) = \{v_{j,\,l}\} \tag{2.4}$$

if the state graphs of the automaton system include the edge $(v_{j,\,l-1}, v_{j,\,l})$ such that $u_{j,\,l} = 'N_i \in Q'$. Hence, $\{v_{j,\,l}\}$ is an element of the set of states, which includes the end nodes of the edges marked as $u = 'N_i'$. Moreover, the element requires that the transition from $\{v_{j,\,l-1}\}$ to $'N_i'$ should be the latest among all the others. The state $'N_i'$ associates with selecting some text to be substituted for the nonterminal N_i. That is the appropriate production, viz. the route j of the automaton A_i is selected.

In order to redefine expressions (2.2), (2.3), and (2.4), in particular, let us perform series of transformations on the state graph of the system S, which do not affect the language being defined.

1. Introduce an additional edge bearing an empty string e for each edge loaded with the nonterminal characters. The additional edge $(v_{j,\,l}, v_{j,\,k})$ with

$u_{j,k} = e$ is introduced if $u_{j,l} \in Q'$ and $u_{j,l+1} \in Q'$ or $v_{j,l} = F_i$. Thus, the following sequence of states: $\{\ldots, v_{j,l}, v_{j,k}, v_{j,l+1}, \ldots\}$ is obtained, i.e. the end node of the "nonterminal" edge will always be the starting node for either the "terminal" edge or the e-edge. The given transformation is also valid if the initial edge of the automaton state graph bears a nonterminal character.

2. Assign to every edge loaded with $u_{j,l} \in T \cup \{e\}$, besides the terminal character, the number s of the route (rule) running from the initial node N_i to the end node F_i and the ordinal edge number of this route. Apply the numbers so that a pair (s, q) will belong only to one edge, i.e. $(s, q)_{j,l}^i = (s, q)_{j',l'}^k$ for $i = k$, $l = l'$ and $j = j'$.

The stacks M and D are intended to save some current information on parsing. The stack M contains the current number of the route, D holds the current number of the edge on this route. The stack alphabet consists of integers. The route number should be sent into the stack if a new route is opened that corresponds to the selection of a new rule. On passing the last edge of the route, its number is deleted from the stack. For each new route registered in the stack M, the stack D saves the last edge number of the route available for transition. Therefore, we will represent the control unit configuration by the quadruple. The third and fourth parameters will associate with the current states of the stacks M and D, respectively. Let us formalize the operations performed while passing the edge (v_1, v_2), which bears a pair of numbers (s, q) and some terminal character a.

$$(v_1, ax, ss', nq') \vdash_A (v_2, x, ss', qq') \tag{2.5}$$

$n = q - 1$ for $q \neq q_{max}$ and $a \in T$, where q_{max} is the maximal edge number of the route s, and $x \in T^* \cup \{e\}$;

$$(v_1, ax, ss', nq') \vdash_A (v_2, x, s', q') \tag{2.6}$$

for $q = q_{max}$; and

$$(v_1, ax, s', q') \vdash_A (v_2, x, ss', qq') \tag{2.7}$$

for $q = 1$.

If the transition takes place along the edge, which is at the same time the first and the last edge of the route, the character is considered admissible and the stack content does not change. Since this edge is the first edge of the route, the pair of numbers should be put into the stack, and since it is simultaneously the last edge the pair of numbers once put into the stack, should be deleted.

$$(v_1, ax, s', q') \underset{A}{\vdash} (v_2, x, s', q') \tag{2.8}$$

For $a = e$ the change of configurations is identical. The transition is possible, if the edge with No. 1 has either an empty string or some terminal character identical to the current character of the input string. So, both stacks M and D are respectively filled in with the route number and the edge number equal to 1. If the edge number of the route selected is maximal, then the stacks M and D unload the current numbers during transition. During transition along the intermediate edge the current number in the stack D increases by 1.

The introduced operations comply with the sequence of states which take place while parsing in accordance with the transition function (2.2). The stacks save the information concerning all the grammar rules involved in parsing the string, which has not been completed yet.

3. Let us examine the edges of the state graph loaded with nonterminal characters. Overlap the state $v_{j,\,l}^k$ with the initial state N_i of the state graph of the automaton A_i if $u_{j,\,l+1}^k = {}'N_i'$. Overlap the final state $v_{i,\,l+1}^k$ of this edge with that of the automaton A_i. The given transformations when performed on all the "nonterminal" edges, make the structures of state graphs of the automaton system be tied together. These links initiate the transitions carried out according to the transition function of the automaton system expressed in (2.3) and (2.4). On binding the ends of "nonterminal" edges when performing the given transformations, these edges can be deleted from the state graph of the automaton system. Now the graph has only the edges loaded with terminals or empty strings.

The grammar of the arithmetic expression $(\{E, F, T\}, \{a, b, *, /, +, -, (,)\}P, E)$ illustrates the given approach. Its productions are

$$E \to T \mid E + T \mid E - T$$
$$T \to F \mid T * F \mid T/F$$
$$F \to a \mid b \mid (E)$$

Let us provide each nonterminal with a state graph of finite-state automaton. See Fig. 2.3 for the state graph of the finite-state automaton $(\{E, F_E, q_1, q_2, q_3, q_4\}, \{+, -, 'T', 'E'\}, t, E, F_E)$ matching the nonterminal E. In the further discussion we will omit the names of intermediate states in state

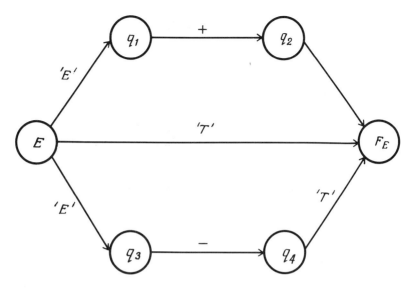

Fig. 2.3. State graph for finite-state automaton A_{E_i}

graphs. Figure 2.4 shows the state graphs for the automatons A_T and A_F constructed in due regard of all the aforesaid. The transition function t is the same for all the mentioned finite-state automatons.

Introduce additional edges and apply numbers to walks and edges in accordance with transformations 1 and 2. See Fig. 2.5 for the obtained graph. A point placed near the edge number indicates the last edge of the walk, which bears the maximal edge number on this walk in the graph.

Transformation 3 suggests that all the edges loaded with nonterminal characters be deleted. Figure 2.6 shows the state graph of the automaton system for the given grammar. As a matter of fact this graph can be considered a state graph of the push-down automaton provided with two stacks. Let us examine the configuration change of such an automaton while identifying the string $a * (a + b) - b$. As the states E, T and F of the graph are merged into one, we will denote it only by E.

$$(E, \ a * (a + b) - b, \ e, \ e) \vdash (F_F, * (a + b) - b, \ e, \ e)$$

On branching along the edge which bears the terminal character a, both walk and edge numbers (7 and 1) put into their stacks are simultaneously deleted, for the given edge is the last on the walk.

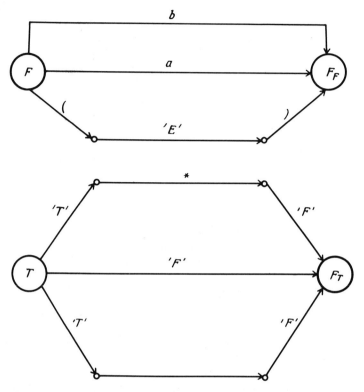

Fig. 2.4. State graphs for finite-state automatons A_T and A_F

$$(F_F, *(a + b) - b, e, e) \vdash (F_T, *(a + b) - b, e, e)$$

Branching along the edge loaded with an empty string is expressed as

$$(F_T, *(a + b) - b, e, e) \vdash (E, (a + b) - b, 5, 1)$$
$$(E, (a + b) - b, 5, 1) \vdash (E, (a + b) - b, 9.5, 1.1)$$

Points separate the numbers stored in stack. Further steps yield

$$\vdash (F_F, +b) - b, 9.5, 1.1)$$
$$\vdash (F_T, +b) - b, 9.5, 1.1)$$
$$\vdash (F_E, +b) - b, 9.5, 1.1)$$
$$\vdash (E, b) - b, 2.9.5, 1.1.1)$$

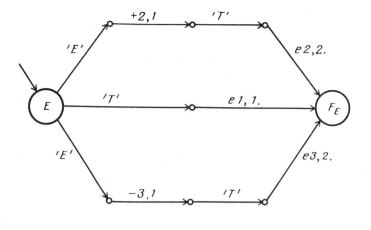

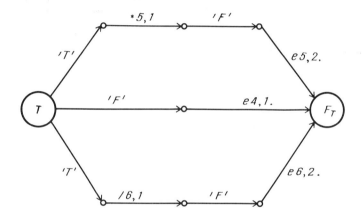

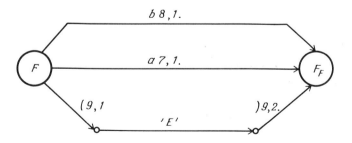

Fig. 2.5. Automaton graphs transformed

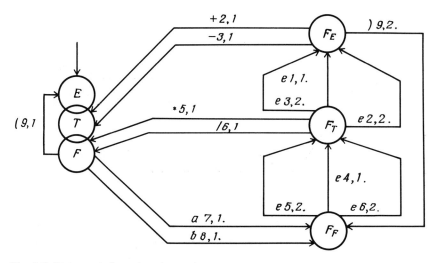

Fig. 2.6. State graph for automaton system

$\vdash (F_F,) - b, 2.9.5, 1.1.1)$

$\vdash (F_T,) - b, 2.9.9.5, 1.1.1)$

$\vdash (F_E,) - b, 9.5, 1.1)$

$\vdash (F_F, -b, 5,1)$

$\vdash (F_T, -b, e, e)$

$\vdash (F_E, -b, e, e)$

$\vdash (E, b, 3, 1)$

$\vdash (F_F, e, 3, 1)$

$\vdash (F_T, e, 3, 1)$

$\vdash (F_E, e, e, e)$

With the deletion of "nonterminal" edges and introduction of two stacks to 33 refine the transition function of the automaton system, the latter can be considered as push-down automaton

$$A = (Q, T, M, t, q_0, m_0, F)$$

where $Q = \bigcup\limits_{i=1}^{Q} Q_i$ = finite set of states

$T = \bigcup\limits_{i=1}^{n} T_i$ = finite input alphabet including terminal characters

and an empty string

M = finite alphabet of stack characters comprising a set of integers and m_0

q_0 = initial state of the push-down automaton (or of the system of automatons)

m_0 = initial stack character (the stack is empty for $m_0 = e$)

F = finite state of the push-down automaton (or of the system of automatons)

t = transition function

$$t : Q \times (T \cup \{e\}) \times M \times M \to R(Q \times M^* \times M^*)$$

The stepping change of configurations inherent in this push-down automaton is identical to that of automaton system expressed in (2.5) through (2.8). If none of the edges is available for transition, then the sentence saved on the input tape does not belong to the language $L(G)$.

Thus, using the transformations suggested it is possible to bind the structures of the state graphs of the separate automatons into the common graph. This enables one to record the transition function in the form of configuration change instead of its general form. For passing over to the common graph no additional restrictions were imposed, therefore, it can be used for parsing context-free languages. The present automaton may not certainly be deterministic for context-free and ATN grammars. Let us define the languages, for which the automaton will be deterministic, and determine the methods of reducing the push-down automaton to its deterministic form.

2.2.   Simple Context-Free Grammars and Languages

Let us examine the avenues of using push-down automatons proceeding from simple languages generated by ATN grammars, context-free s- and q-grammars. The restrictions imposed enable one to construct deterministic identifiers by means of traditional techniques.

ATN Grammars

As already mentioned, the productions $v \rightarrow w$ of ATN grammar $G = (N, T, P, S)$ comply with the restrictions of the form $v \in N$, $w \in T \times N$ or $w \in T$. In the general case, the state graph of the automaton system matching this grammar consists of the routes, which connect the initial and final nodes of automatons. Note that all the initial and end vertices of the resulting graph are detached. None of the vertices (N_i) will merge with another one, for all the grammar rules begin with terminal characters. Therefore, no graphs will contain an initial edge bearing a nonterminal. The end vertices (F_i) of the state graph are always isolated for all types of grammars.

The edges loaded with empty strings and always bearing No. 2 will rise from the vertices F_i of the state graph, which associate with the finite states of the automaton system. The right-hand part of the production includes the only nonterminal which is its second and the last character. Thus the edges under No. 1 are incident out of the N_i, and those under No. 2 are incident out of the nodes F_i. The state graph does not contain any other nodes.

Let us discuss four schemes of configuration changes for the automaton system. They can be implemented in agreement with expressions (2.6), (2.7) and (2.8). Passing the first and the last edges complies with expressions (2.7) and (2.6), respectively. Passing the single edge (for $a = e$) associates with expression (2.8). The selection of an edge incident out of the vertex F_i is always unique because the edges under No. 2 incident out of F_i belong to different routes. The graph cannot contain two No. 2 edges with the same walk number. Nonidentity of the pairs of numbers can be attributed to the techniques of applying numbers to the edges in constructing the state graph. Thus, the edge selected should bear the same walk number as the number at the top of the stack M.

The edge for the transition from the vertex N_i is selected with consideration of both the terminal character on the edge and the current character on the input tape. So, two edges incident out of some vertex of the state graph, when loaded with identical terminals, make the state graph indeterministic. Such a situation is not ruled out in ATN grammars. Later on we shall consider reduction of an indeterministic state graph to the deterministic form. Now let us discuss the ATN grammar $G = (\{B, C, D\}, \{a, b, c, d\}, P, B)$ with the productions

$$B \rightarrow bC \mid d$$
$$C \rightarrow cC \mid bD$$
$$D \rightarrow a$$

The state graphs of some automatons are shown in Fig. 2.7a.

Figure 2.7b illustrates the deterministic state graph of the system of automatons. Note that it is redundant if compared to the state graph of the push-down automaton for the same grammar considered in Chapter 1 (see Fig. 1.13). All its finite states are combined into one. Identifying the string bba causes the following change in the configurations:

$$(B, \ bba, \ e, \ e) \ \vdash \ (C, \ bb, \ 1.1)$$
$$\vdash \ (D, \ a, \ 4.1, \ 1.1)$$
$$\vdash \ (F_D, \ e, \ 4.1, \ 1.1)$$
$$\vdash \ (F_C, \ e, \ 1, \ 1)$$
$$\vdash \ (F_B, \ e, \ e, \ e)$$

Thus, we have found an approach usable for parsing ATN languages. As for the finite-state automaton the determinacy of the state graph depends upon the grammar type.

Context-Free s-Grammars

The given grammar is similar to ATN grammar, for the right-hand parts of its productions begin with terminal characters. The grammar productions are of the form $v \to w$, where $v \in N$, $w \in (T \cup N)^+$, or more exactly $w \in T \times (T \cup N)^*$. If two productions $v \to x_1 w$ and $v \to x_2 w'$ exist, then it is imperative that $x_1 = x_2$.

The analysis of constructing a state graph for the automaton system reveals that the graph for the s-grammar can contain some intermediate states besides N_i and F_i. Constructing the graph implies that only one edge leaves the intermediate state. Thus, there is no need to select edges in such vertexes.

The edges with No. 1 loaded with terminal characters rise from the initial vertex N_i as in ATN grammars. The edge can also be selected unambiguously for such a vertex, because the edges incident out of each vertex N_i have different terminal characters. This follows directly from the restrictions imposed on the productions of s-grammar. Let us find out wether for the vertex F_i the choice of the edge is unique in changing the configuration of the automaton system. Note that the numbers of the edges leaving F_i are greater than 1, because the first numbers have been assigned to the edges incident out of N_i. Transformation 2 of the state graph being constructed implies that the edges leaving the vertex F_i cannot have identical numbers of both the path

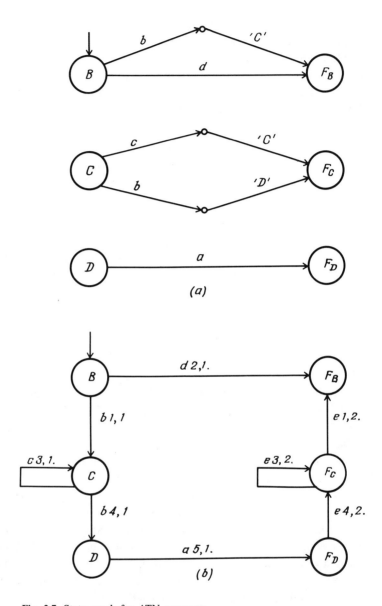

Fig. 2.7. State graph for ATN grammar

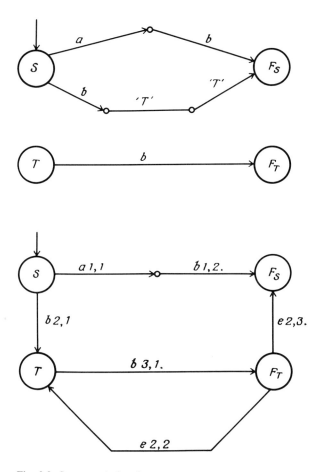

Fig. 2.8. State graph for S-grammar

and the edge. The edge should be selected according to the numbers of the path and edge at the top of the stacks M and D, respectively. Hence, selecting the edges is unique even in spite of identical terminal characters loaded.

Figure 2.8 shows the state graph constructed for the grammar $G = (\{S, T\}, \{a, b\}, P, S)$. Its productions are

$$S \rightarrow ab \mid bTT$$
$$T \rightarrow b$$

The following change of configurations involves identification of the string bbb:

$$(S, \ bbb, \ e, \ e) \vdash (T, \ bb, \ 2, \ 1)$$
$$\vdash (F_T, \ b, \ 2, \ 1)$$
$$\vdash (T, \ b, \ 2, \ 2)$$
$$\vdash (F_T, \ e, \ 2, \ 2)$$
$$\vdash (F_S, \ e, \ e, \ e)$$

Note that two edges of the same path loaded with empty strings leave the node F_T. One edge is selected according to its number at the top of the stack D. Expressions (2.5) and (2.6) imply that the transition is performed along the edge with a number, which is unit greater than that at the top of the stack D. Thus, it can be concluded that the state graph of the automaton system is deterministic for s-grammars.

Context-Free q-Grammars

The following restrictions are imposed on q-grammar productions:

$$v \in N, \ w \in T \times (T \cup N)^* \ \text{or} \ w = e$$

That is, the right-hand part of q-grammar production, $v \to w$ can either begin with a terminal character or be an empty string e. Unlike s-grammar, the right-hand parts of q-grammar productions can contain empty strings e. It is sufficient for s-grammar that the productions with the identical left-hand parts begin with different terminal characters. However q-grammar requires some extension of the condition: the selection sets of productions having the same left-hand parts should be disjoint.

The state graphs of the automaton system for both q- and s-grammar have the same traits. Introduce the edge loaded with an empty string. This edge is always labeled 1 and is incident out of the vertex N_i. Such an edge is unique for each nonterminal N_i, because only one rule $N_i \to e$ can exist for each value of i. Since all the edges $(N_i, \ \ldots)$ have different terminal characters, the edge available for the transition can uniquely be selected. If the transition along one such edge is possible, then this must be performed. However, why is not the transition along the empty edge performed first, though it is always possible? Suppose that the productions $N_i \to a$ and $N_i \to e$ were involved in the construction of the automaton A_i. From the q-grammar definition it follows that the selection sets of productions are disjoint, i.e. $a \notin CH(N_i \to e) = FL(N_i)$. Put another way, the empty edge will never be followed by edge No. 1 with the terminal a. That is why, if possible, the transition along the edge bearing a terminal character is always performed first. If there is no such edge, then the empty edge should be passed last. If the latter edge is also absent, parsing the input string is terminated and the input string is not considered belonging to the language $L(G)$.

The edge leaving the vertex F_i is selected in the same manner as for s-grammars. Hence the state graph for the automaton system is deterministic for q-grammars as well.

Let us consider the grammar $G = (\{S, A\}, \{a, b, c\}, P, S)$ with the productions

$$S \to aAS \mid b$$
$$A \to cAS \mid e$$

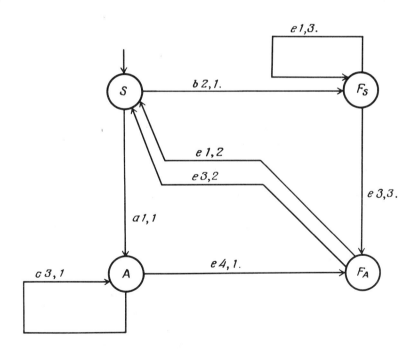

Fig. 2.9. State graph for q-grammar

Figure 2.9 illustrates the state graph of this grammar. Identify the string *acbb* as follows:

$$(S, \; acbb, \; e, \; e) \vdash (A, \; cbb, \; 1, \; 1)$$
$$\vdash (A, \; bb, \; 3.1, \; 1.1)$$
$$\vdash (F_A, \; bb, \; 3.1, \; 1.1)$$
$$\vdash (S, \; bb, \; 3.1, \; 2.1)$$
$$\vdash (F_S, \; b, \; 3.1, \; 2.1)$$
$$\vdash (F_A, \; b, \; 1, \; 1)$$
$$\vdash (S, \; b, \; 1, \; 2)$$
$$\vdash (F_S, \; e, \; 1, \; 2)$$
$$\vdash (F_s, \; e, \; e, \; e)$$

We have considered the most simple grammars. Using the suggested approach enables one to organize deterministic parsing of the languages generated by *s*- and *q*-grammars. We now pursue our studying context-free languages gradually lifting the restrictions imposed on the forms of productions.

2.3.   Parsing *LL*(*k*)- and *LR*(*k*)-languages

LL(1)-grammars

An *LL*(1)-grammar allows the nonterminals to precede the right-hand parts of its productions. The principal restriction imposed on the form of productions requires that the sets of directive characters for the rules with identical left-hand parts should not intersect.

The presence of nonterminals at the beginning of the right-hand parts of the productions promotes merging of the initial vertexes N_i of the automatons in the state graph transformed. Let us analyze wether the *LL*(1)-grammar admits two merged vertexes to give rise to the edges loaded with identical terminal characters. Suppose that the grammar has generated the productions $A \to a$ ... and $C \to a$ ... with their vertexes A and C merged in the transformed graph (Fig. 2.10). To make the vertexes merge, introduce the production of the form $X \to A \mid C$. However, this is not consistent with the *LL*(1)-grammar.

Another approach to merging the vertexes becomes possible in the presence of two grammar productions having different left-hand parts which contain

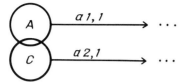

Fig. 2.10. Union of vertexes in state graph

one and the same nonterminal character (say, *B*),

$$D \to A \mid B \dots$$
$$X \to C \mid B \dots$$
$$S \to aD \mid bX$$

The example considered complies with the *LL* (1)-grammar. Figure 2.11 shows a fragment of its state graph for the automaton system. Basing on the above example, it can be concluded that *LL* (1)-grammars admit the edges bearing the same terminals to leave the groups of initial vertexes. Substituting the rule $C \to e$ for $C \to a$ produces one more type of indeterminacy of the present grammar.

Insert an empty string *e* into the above grammar.

$$A \to a \dots$$
$$C \to a \dots$$
$$D \to A \mid B \dots$$

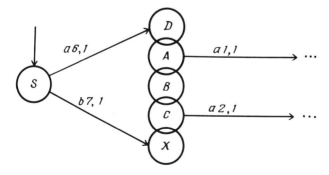

Fig. 2.11. Fragment of state graph for *LL* (1)-grammar

$$X \to C \mid eB \ldots$$
$$B \to b \ldots$$
$$S \to aD \mid bX$$

A fragment of the state graph for this grammar is shown in Fig. 2.12. Here the group of vertexes is obviously separated and the selection of edges is deterministic. Nonetheless, inserting the edge with an empty string may cause several edges labeled 1 to be incident out of the same vertex. Thus, the form of indeterminacy has changed.

Consider the end vertexes of the state graph constructed for the *LL* (1)-grammar. Try to find out wether two edges loaded either with the identical terminals or the empty strings can be incident out of the end vertex simultaneously (Fig. 2.13). Here, a grammar fragment for the mentioned state graph may appear as

$$X \to AaB \ldots$$
$$Y \to AaC \ldots$$
$$A \to b$$

The nonterminals X and Y can be present either separately in the right-hand parts of different productions or together in the same right-hand part of the

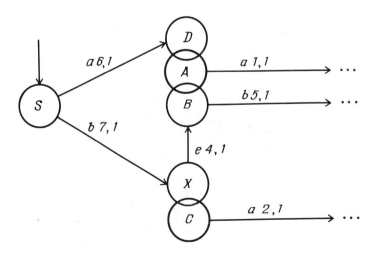

Fig. 2.12. Fragment of state graph with "empty" edges

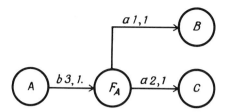

Fig. 2.13. Fragment of state graph with end vertexes

production. For example, the production $D \rightarrow bXY$ is consistent with the
LL (1)-grammar definition. Thus, the state graphs for LL (1)-grammars can
have the edges under No. 1 loaded with the terminal characters which are incident out of the end vertexes.

Let us substitute an empty string e for the terminal a in the grammar discussed. We get

$$X \rightarrow ABx$$
$$Y \rightarrow ACy$$
$$A \rightarrow b$$
$$D \rightarrow bXY$$

Figure 2.14 shows a fragment of the state graph of the automaton system
constructed for this grammar. As is seen the edges labeled 1 bearing empty
strings can also be incident out of one and the same end vertex F. Routing
is ambiguous for such edges.

Let us examine the case when the edges labeled 1 are loaded with both

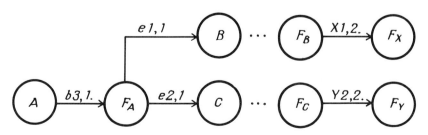

Fig. 2.14. Fragment of state graph with "empty" edges rising from end vertexes

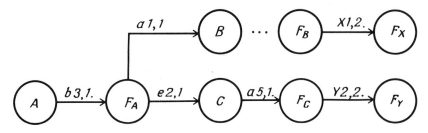

Fig. 2.15. Fragment of state graph with "empty" and "terminal" edges

empty strings and terminal characters,

$$X \rightarrow AaBx$$
$$Y \rightarrow ACy$$
$$A \rightarrow b$$
$$D \rightarrow bXY$$
$$C \rightarrow a$$

Taking account of the current character a on the input tape, we choose unambiguously any of the two edges, (F_A, B) or (F_A, C), available for the transition (Fig. 2.15).

Consider the LL (1)-grammar with the productions

$$X \rightarrow AB$$
$$Y \rightarrow yACc$$
$$Z \rightarrow zAD$$
$$M \rightarrow X \mid Y \mid Z$$
$$A \rightarrow b$$

The state graph of this grammar is shown in Fig. 2.16. Suppose that the automaton system is in the state F_A, the stacks M and D hold respectively 2 and 1 at their tops, and the reading head indicates the current character a. So, which edge should be chosen for the transition, (F_A, B) or (F_A, C)? The edge (F_A, B) labeled 1 indicates that the nonterminal character A appears first in some productions $X \rightarrow AB$. The edge (F_A, C) points to that the production has been already selected in accordance with the terminal character y, and routing (A, F_A) is currently taking place. Since the routing of (A, F_A) does not include the edge (F_A, B), we are to execute transition along (F_A, C). The

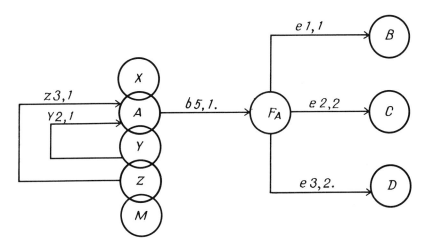

Fig. 2.16. Fragment of state graph with edges bearing different numbers and "empty" string

path (A, F_A) may comprise the edge (F_A, B) if the grammar contains the production $A \rightarrow AB$, i.e. it is left-recursive grammar. However, left-recursive grammars do not belong to *LL* (1)-grammars. Therefore, for the latter grammars, the transitions are performed along the edges whose numbers are greater than 1. Though the edge labeled 1 can have a terminal and be available for the transition (substitute $X \rightarrow AaB$ for $X \rightarrow AB$), the edge with the number greater than 1 is preferred. If both edges are loaded with the terminal a, the transition is performed along the edge (F_A, C).

Finally, we can conclude that the state graph of the automaton system for *LL* (1)-grammars is indeterministic. We list the types of ambiguous selection of edges available for transitions in indeterministic graphs. Suppose two edges (a, b) and (a, c), are respectively loaded with $P_{(a, b)} = x$ and $P_{(a, c)} = y$ and are incident out of the same vertex a. Selecting the edge in the vertex a will be ambiguous under the following conditions.

1. Each of the two edges is labeled 1 and loaded with an identical terminal,

$$x = \{a, n, 1\}, y = \{a, m, 1\}, m \neq n$$

2. Each of the two edges is labeled and loaded with an empty string,

$$x = \{e, n, 1\}, y = \{e, m, 1\}$$

3. One edge is loaded with a terminal, $x = \{a, n, 1\}$, the other with an empty string, $y = \{e, m, 1\}$.

Figure 2.17 shows the state graph of the automaton system for the LL (1)-grammar

$$(\{S, F, E, A, B\}, \{a, +, *\}, P, S)$$

with the productions

$$S \rightarrow AE$$
$$E \rightarrow +AE \mid e$$
$$A \Rightarrow FB$$
$$B \rightarrow *FB \mid e$$
$$F \rightarrow a \mid (S)$$

Examining the vertexes B and E of the graph reveals the third type of indeterminacy. So far as we deal with the LL (1)-grammar, and the initial vertexes

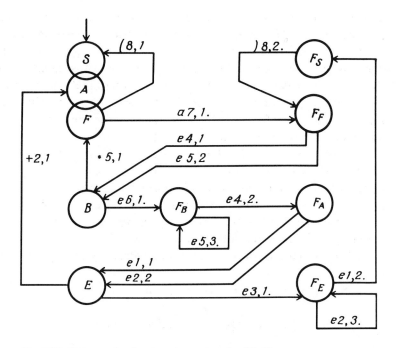

Fig. 2.17. State graph of automaton system for LL (1)-grammar

B and *E* are separate, we prefer the edges with the terminals. In view of the above-said the graph is deterministic. In identifying the string $a * (a + a)$, the configurations change as follows:

$$(S, \ a * (a + a), \ e, \ e) \vdash (F_F, \ * (a + a), \ e, \ e)$$
$$\vdash (B, \ * (a + a), \ 4, \ 1)$$
$$\vdash (F, \ (a + a), \ 5.4, \ 1.1)$$
$$\vdash (S, \ a + a), \ 8.5, \ 4, \ 1.1.1)$$
$$\vdash (F_F, \ +a), \ 8.5.4, \ 1.1.1)$$
$$\vdash (B, \ +a), \ 4.8.5.4, \ 1.1.1.1)$$
$$\vdash (F_B, \ +a), \ 4.8.5.4, \ 1.1.1.1)$$
$$\vdash (F_A, \ +a), \ 8.5.4, \ 1.1.1)$$
$$\vdash (E, \ +a), \ 1.8.5.4, \ 1.1.1.1)$$
$$\vdash (A, \ a), \ 2.1.8.5.4, \ 1.1.1.1.1)$$
$$\vdash (F_F,), \ 2.1.8.5.4, \ 1.1.1.1.1)$$
$$\vdash (B,), \ 4.2.1.8.5.4, \ 1.1.1.1.1.1)$$
$$\vdash (F_B,), \ 4.2.1.8.5.4, \ 1.1.1.1.1.1)$$
$$\vdash (F_A,), \ 2.1.8.5.4, \ 1.1.1.1.1)$$
$$\vdash (E,), \ 2.1.8.5.4, \ 2.1.1.1.1)$$
$$\vdash (F_E,), \ 2.1.8.5.4, \ 2.1.1.1.1)$$
$$\vdash (F_E,), \ 1.8.5.4, \ 1.1.1.1)$$
$$\vdash (F_S,), \ 8.5.4, \ 1.1.1)$$
$$\vdash (F_F, \ e, \ 5.4, \ 1.1)$$
$$\vdash (B, \ e, \ 5.4, \ 2.1)$$
$$\vdash (F_B, \ e, \ 5.4, \ 2.1)$$
$$\vdash (F_B, \ e, \ 4, \ 1)$$
$$\vdash (F_A, \ e, \ e, \ e)$$
$$\vdash (E, \ e, \ 1, \ 1)$$
$$\vdash (F_E, \ e, \ 1, \ 1)$$
$$\vdash (F_S, \ e, \ e, \ e)$$

LL (*k*)-Grammars

The *LL* (1)-grammar discussed in the previous subsection is a particular case of *LL* (*k*)-grammars for $k = 1$. We show that all types of indeterminacy discussed above can be extended to *LL* (*k*)-grammars.

Consider the production $A \rightarrow w$. The left-hand derivation

$$S \overset{*}{\Rightarrow} yAv \Rightarrow ywv \Rightarrow yx \in T^*$$

implies that unambiguous choice of the substitution $A \rightarrow wv$, $w \in (N \cup T)^*$ is possible if at least k characters of the input tape are scanned. The state graph matching such a grammar provides two or several routes originating from the state A with $(k - 1)$ identical characters. Figure 2.18 shows a fragment of such a graph. The initial legs of the paths $(A, D, \ldots)$, $(A, M, F_M, \ldots)$, $(A, B, C, \ldots)$ include the same characters a and c. Selecting one of the edges $(A, \ldots)$ incident out of the node A depends on the information held in stacks and assigned to the edges $(A, \ldots)$ of the state graph. It also depends on the current character or the character group saved on the input tape. Making a decision on routing takes account only of the initial edges and their loads. Other edges of the paths are ignored. While studying the types of indeterminacy, attention is exclusively paid to the first edges of the paths $(A, \ldots)$ and no restrictions are imposed on the loads of subsequent edges

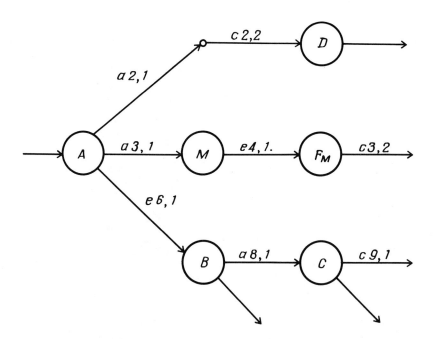

Fig. 2.18. Fragment of state graph for LL (k)-grammar

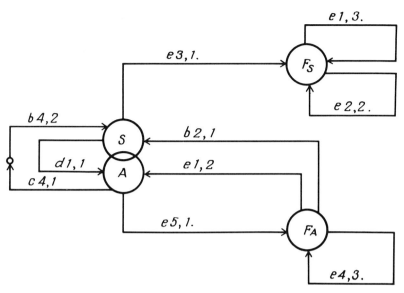

Fig. 2.19. State graph for *LL* (2)-grammar

of the routes (A, F_A). That is why the types of indeterminacy for the state graphs inherent in *LL* (k)-grammars are the same as those in *LL* (1)-grammars.

Figure 2.19 shows the state graph for the *LL* (2)-grammar $G = (\{S, A\}, \{d, b, c\}, P, S)$. The set P of this grammar comprises the following productions:

$$S \rightarrow dAS \mid AbS \mid e$$
$$A \rightarrow cbA \mid d$$

The choice of the edge for the state S is ambiguous. There are four edges labeled 1; one of them is loaded with an empty string. Two edges have the same terminals. This implies that the state graph of Fig. 2.19 is not applicable for non-reset parsing.

LR (*k*)-Grammars

The definition of *LR* (*k*)-grammars proceeds from the right-hand derivation of sentences of a language. The suggested approach to parsing as applied to the state graph of the automaton system involves the left-hand derivation techniques. Using different schemes of derivations does not permit of obtaining any new information on the state graph's indeterminacy from the restrictions imposed on $LR(k)$-grammars. Therefore, we resume discussing context-free grammars without imposing any restrictions on it. To this end, consider some examples given below.

Construct a state graph for the $LL(2)$-grammar

$$G = (\{S,\ A,\ B\},\ \{a,\ ,\ ,\ b\},\ P,\ S)$$

with the productions

$$S \rightarrow A,\ S \mid A$$
$$A \rightarrow aB$$
$$B \rightarrow b \mid b,\ B$$

Having examined the graph of Fig. 2.20, it can be inferred that the selection of the edge in the state B is ambiguous. Neither the character b nor the string b, if present on the input tape, will help to choose one of the two edges avail-

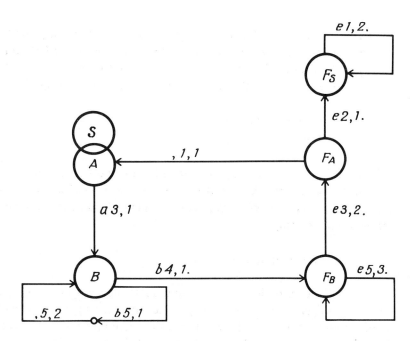

Fig. 2.20. State graph for $LR(2)$-grammar

able in this state for further parsing. Here, we deal with the first type of indeterminacy, which falls into those concerning *LL* (1)-grammars.

Another illustrative example is the left-recursive grammar

$$G = (\{A,\ X,\ Y,\ Z,\ S,\ B,\ C,\ D\},\ \{a,\ z,\ b,\ d\},\ P,\ S)$$

with the productions

$$X \to AB \dots$$
$$Y \to AaC \dots$$
$$Z \to zAD \dots$$
$$A \to Aa \mid b \mid dA$$
$$S \to X \mid Y \mid Z$$

The state graph for this grammar is shown in Fig. 2.21. This type of indeterminacy is not among those of *LL* (1) grammars. Neither the edge (F_A, D) nor any of the edges $(F_A, \dots)$ labeled 1 can be unambiguously chosen. Really, since left recursion is admitted, opening a new path labeled 4 entails the substitution of the nonterminal A in the string zaD including the production $A \to Aa$. At the same time, we cannot recognize left recursion in examining

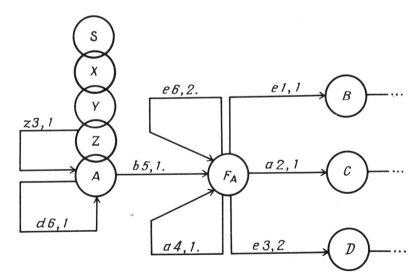

Fig. 2.21. Fragment of state graph for left-recursive grammar

these edges. Based only on the edges $(F_A, \ldots)$ of the state graph, it cannot be said whether (F_A, F_A) or (F_A, C) results from left recursion. Hence the choice of an edge in the vertex F is ambiguous. The situation would not change if the edge (F_A, D) were loaded with terminals.

Based on the obtained results, we can find the types of indeterminacy inherent in state graphs for context-free grammars. Suppose that there exist the edges (a, b) and (a, c) loaded respectively with predicates x and y. Selecting an edge in the vertex a is ambiguous if:

(a) both edges are loaded with identical terminals and one of the edges is labeled 1,

$$x = \{a, n, 1\}, \ y = \{a, m, l\}, \ m \neq n, \ l \geqslant 1$$

(b) both edges are loaded with empty strings and one of the edges is labeled 1,

$$x = \{e, n, 1\}, \ y = \{e, m, l\}, \ m \neq n, \ l \geqslant 1$$

(c) one edge is loaded with an empty string, the other with a terminal and one of the edges is labeled 1,

$$x = \{a, n, 1\}, \ y = \{e, m, l\} \text{ or } x = \{e, n, 1\},$$
$$y = \{a, m, l\}, \ m \neq n, \ l \geqslant 1$$

All the above variants are met for the end vertexes of the graphs. For the initial vertexes, each of two edges incident out of such a vertex is always labeled 1, i.e. $l = 1$. Thus, we have found out that the state graph for a context-free grammar is nondeterministic and have analyzed the cases of ambiguous selection of the edges. Now let us try to reduce this graph to deterministic form.

2.4.   Reducing a State Graph to Deterministic Form

In transforming graphs, we adhere to the main principle: the language admitted by the automaton system must not suffer any changes. Therefore, deleting, replacing, and introducing new edges should not give rise to any complementary paths and make any of existing paths escape. Let us analyze all the types of indeterminacy revealed earlier.

Take the edges loaded with empty strings to begin with the analysis, and those with terminals to continue. Pay special attention to edges-loops. Transformations reducing the number of edges and simultaneously increasing their loads will complete our discussion.

Deleting "Empty" Edges

The first and most simple way to transform a graph is to delete the edges loaded with empty strings e or to reduce their number. Let us take the edge with an empty string, which is the only edge of the path (Fig. 2.22a). The edge $(A, 2)$ is the first and sole edge of the path m. Such an edge can be incident out of initial and terminal vertexes of the state graph. Neither the stack content changes nor the indicator shifts along the input tape on routing the given edge. Therefore, we can delete this edge (Fig. 2.22b) and use the edges incident out of vertex 2 instead.

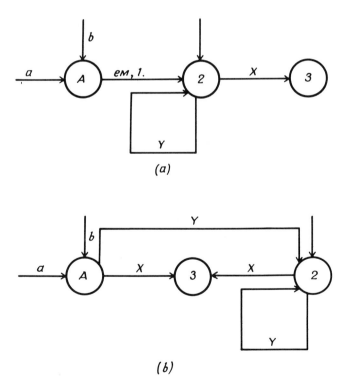

Fig. 2.22. Deleting an edge loaded with empty string

Referring to the original graph illustrated in Fig. 2.22*a*, it can be seen that after routing the edge (*A*, 2) two edges, (2, 2) or (2, 3), are available for parsing. Therefore, the deleted edge is replaced by the edges (*A*, 2) and (*A*, 3) bearing the predicates *x* and *y*, respectively (Fig. 2.22*b*). Routing these edges is equivalent to routing the paths (*A*, 2, 2) and (*A*, 2, 3) of the graph shown in Fig. 2.22*a*. The edges (2, 2) and (2, 3) shown in Fig. 2.22*a* are also present in the graph of Fig. 2.22*b*, for the edges of other paths are incident into vertex 2. If no edges are incident into vertex 2 and it has only the outgoing edges, then this vertex can be deleted. Such a vertex would never become current when parsing.

Transforming a state graph of automaton system can give rise to edges-loops loaded with empty strings. Such an edge-loop (F_A, F_A) is shown in Fig. 2.23. Deletion or any transformation of such edges may cause difficulties. Let us consider various grammars and appropriate state graphs where such edges can be met with.

Suppose we deal with the initial edge of the path incident out of the vertex F_A of the automaton system. This situation may arise only in the case of the production of the form $A \to eA \ldots$. However, such productions enable deletion of the initial dummy character before constructing the state graph, because practically it does not affect the sentences of the language. The language processor designers take no account of dummy characters present in sentences, and are interested only in the terminals of sentences.

Constructing the state graph implies that the edge-loop can never be incident out of an intermediate vertex. So we are to discuss only the end vertexes

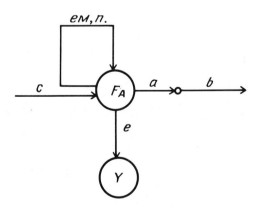

Fig. 2.23. Edge-loop bearing empty string

of the graph. Thus, F_A is an end vertex (see Fig. 2.23), i.e. the production of the form $A \rightarrow \dots A$ exists such that the nonterminal A is the last character of its right-hand part. Hence the edge $(\dots, F_A)$ is the last edge of the route. The edge $(F_A, \dots)$ labeled 1 makes the selection of the edge in the vertex F_A ambiguous. This variant exists when the grammar contains productions of the form $X \rightarrow Aab \dots, X \rightarrow AY \dots$, or $A \rightarrow Aab \dots$. The analysis of the first two productions shows that the edge-loop should be routed first, for this completes substitution of the nonterminal A. The third production being left-recursive requires that, if possible, routing the edge with the terminal a be executed prior to routing the edge-loop. Therefore, it is advisable to arrange in the following order the edges leaving the end vertexes. Start with the edges labeled of left-recursive productions, place the edges-loops next, and then arrange the edges of nonleft-recursive productions. The initial edge $(F_A, \dots)$ loaded with $x, n, 1$ is associated with the left-recursive production if $(\dots, F_A)$ is the last edge of the path n.

The commonly encountered state graph is shown in Fig. 2.24a. Figure 2.22 illustrates its particular case. It admits the edge $(A, 2)$ loaded with the empty string $e, m, k, k = 1$ and this is the only edge on the route m. In other cases, the transformation of graphs is almost analogous except for the cases dealing with complex loads.

On routing the edge $(A, 2)$ Fig. (2.24a), further parsing can involve any edge $(2, \dots)$, if it is the last on the path m. Otherwise, the edges loaded with $\dots, m, k + 1$ or $\dots, \dots, 1$ are involved. The group of edges is substituted for the edge $(A, 2)$. Introduce a new edge (A, x) for each edge $(2, x)$ along which parsing can be continued. The load of the new edge is composed of those on the edge to be replaced and the edge $(2, x)$ (Fig. 2.24b). The load elements are separated by semicolon.

Routing the edge having a complex load is always accompanied by a change in configurations. The configurations spell one another in accordance with each component of the complex load. For example, routing the edge $(A, 2)$ (Fig. 2.24b) causes the following change in configurations:

$$(A, yab, m.s', k - 1.q') \vdash (\dots, yab, m.s', k.q')$$
$$(\dots, yab, m.s', k.q') \vdash (2, ab, m.s', k + 1.q')$$

for $m = q, j = k + 1, k \neq 1$, or

$$(A, yab, m.s', k - 1.q') \vdash (\dots, yab, m.s', k.q')$$
$$(\dots, yab, m.s', k.q') \vdash (2, ab, q.m.s', 1.k.q')$$

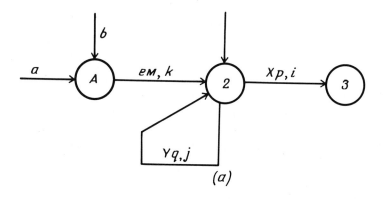

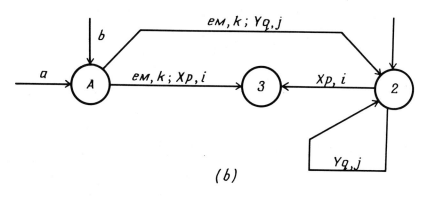

Fig. 2.24. Substitution for intermediate or initial "empty" edge

for $m \neq q$, $j = 1$, $k \neq 1$, or

$$(A,\ yab,\ s',\ q') \vdash (\ldots,\ yab,\ m.s',\ 1.q')$$
$$(\ldots,\ yab,\ m.s',\ 1.q') \vdash (2,\ ab,\ q.m.s',\ 1.1.q')$$

for $m \neq q$, $k = 1$, $j = 1$.

The change of configurations can be re-written in a concise form as

$$(A,\ yab,\ m.s',\ k - 1.q') \vdash (2,\ ab,\ m.s',\ k + 1.q'),\ m = q,$$
$$k \neq 1,\ j = k + 1,\ \text{or}$$
$$(A,\ yab,\ m.s',\ k - 1.q') \vdash (2,\ ab,\ q.m.s',\ 1.k.q'),\ m \neq q,$$
$$k \neq 1,\ j = 1,\ \text{or}$$
$$(A,\ yab,\ s',\ q') \vdash (2,\ ab,\ q.m.s',\ 1.1.q'),\ m \neq q,\ k = 1,\ j = 1$$

Using the above techniques of deleting the empty edges is not advantageous for the first edges of the paths, which have common initial and terminal vertexes (Fig. 2.25a). These edges will combine with a great number of identical edges. That is why by the end of transformation they will not differ from each other. Hence, these edges should be first transformed (see Fig. 2.25b) and then the empty edges should be deleted.

Let us transform the edge (X, Y). In so doing, a new route n is introduced. The first edge (X, Y) of this route bears an empty string and is disposed at the place of the edges being transformed. The mentioned edge corresponds to (F_A, B) loaded with $en, 1$ in the above example. Now introduce a new vertex F_Z and another terminal edge (F_Y, F_Z) of the route n bearing the empty string $en, 2$. The initial vertex of the edges $(F_Y, \ldots)$ of the paths whose first dummy edges are deleted is transferred from F_Y to F_Z. Thus the numbers of all the rest edges decrease by one. Figure 2.25b shows these transformations for the edges (F_B, B).

To substantiate the given transformations, we shall prove their equivalence

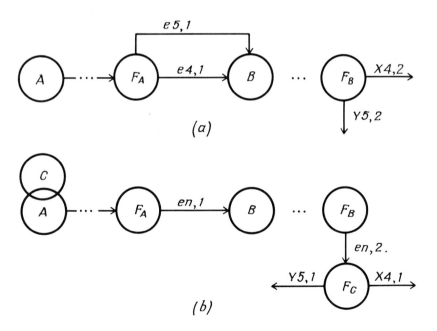

Fig. 2.25. Substitution for "empty" edges having the same vertexes

to introducing a nonterminal into the grammar to reveal the common part of two productions. Consider the productions

$$D \rightarrow ABx$$
$$E \rightarrow ABy$$

Shown in Fig. 2.25a is a fragment of the appropriate state graph. Let the nonterminal C denote the common part of the above productions to get the productions of the form

$$D \rightarrow Cx$$
$$E \rightarrow Cy$$
$$C \rightarrow AB$$

Figure 2.25b illustrates a fragment of the corresponding state graph. We can omit the additional notation of the vertex A as C. The empty edges can be deleted following the earlier mentioned procedure.

Now, we are only to find out whether the transformations discussed remove all the empty edges from the state graph. Suppose there exists an empty edge (A, B) and no edge is incident out of the vertex B except for empty edges-loops. Such a vertex cannot be initial, or else the grammar should contain at least one production of the form $B \rightarrow \ldots$. Such a production, if exists, has its right-hand part at least in the form of an empty string, i.e. the graph contains some edge. If the right-hand parts of nonrecursive productions include the nonterminal B, then some edge can be incident out of the vertex $\ldots B$. Presume that there exists a production of the form $B \rightarrow \ldots B$. Thus, the nonterminal B can only be present in such productions and is not included in the right-hand parts of productions of other nonterminals. It can be inferred that this nonterminal is the initial grammar character, i.e. the grammar contains one such finite state. Therefore, the graph when transformed, can comprise the empty edges which enter the finite state, besides the empty edges-loops. Of course, transition along such edges is performed last.

Transforming Terminal Edges

We have discussed the types of indeterminacy when one or two edges are loaded with empty strings. Now we pass over to examining the edges which bear terminals, i.e. the first type of indeterminacy. Because empty edges have been removed from the graph, the second type of indeterminacy cannot take place. No conflict occurs between the remaining empty edges and those loaded with terminals (i.e. the third type of indeterminacy), because we have managed to assign priorities to these edges. To resolve the conflict between the edges bearing identical terminals, the information loaded in these edges is evidently insufficient. Therefore, we transform the edges increasing their loads till their unambiguous selection becomes possible.

Consider separately the initial and end vertexes. Suppose two edges (X, Y) loaded each with the terminal a are incident out of one and the same vertex X and enter the end vertex Y. The analysis of the state graph construction process may permit of formulating a number of restrictions imposed on the end vertex of these edges. The vertex Y must be the initial vertex of some automaton of the system. It cannot be an intermediate vertex by its construction, because each production corresponds to a separate path and one edge is incident into the intermediate vertex.

Let the node Y be the end vertex of an automaton of the system. This is the node F_X, for the edge incident out of the initial vertex can enter an initial vertex of some other automaton, an intermediate or an end vertex of its own automaton. We can assume that there exist a pair of edges (X, F_X) loaded with the terminal a. This implies that the grammar has generated two identical rules of the form $X \rightarrow a$ — which makes no sense. Now, it can be inferred that if X is the initial vertex of the automaton, then Y is the initial vertex as well.

Discuss the case when $X \neq Y$. The grammar contains two rules: $X \rightarrow aYx \ldots$ and $X \rightarrow aYy \ldots$. Any characters including nonterminals can be substituted for the terminals x and y.

Having introduced the new rule $Z \rightarrow aY$, we can rewrite the previous rules as $X \rightarrow Zx \ldots, X \rightarrow Zy \ldots$. Constructing the state graph will produce a new automaton Z with the vertexes Z and F_Z. Its only path is (Z, F_Z). Let us apply number n to this path. Constructing the state graph makes the vertex Z merge with the vertex X and gives rise to the sole edge (X, Y) loaded with an, 1. The empty edge (F_Y, F_Z) is the second and the last edge on the path n. The two edges $(F_Y, \ldots)$ loaded with xk, 2 and yl, 2 will be replaced with the edges $(F_Z, \ldots)$ loaded with xk, 1 and yl, 1. The numbers of all the edges left on the paths k and l will decrease by 1. Figure 2.26a and b shows the graph with the edges (X, Y) and the graph already transformed. The empty edge that has appeared can be deleted, if necessary following the above described procedure. The resulting graph is shown in Fig. 2.26c.

Analogous transformations take place for $X = Y$, i.e. both edges are loops

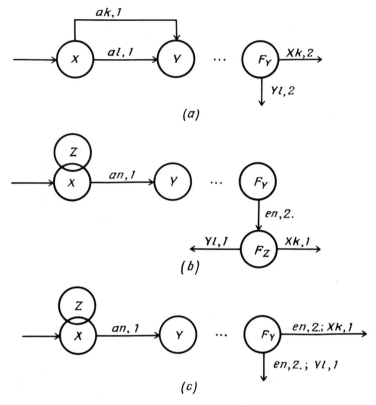

Fig. 2.26. Substitution for edges having the same vertexes and bearing terminal characters

(X, X) (Fig. 2.27a). The productions

$$X \rightarrow aXx\ldots$$
$$X \rightarrow aXy\ldots$$

can be reduced to the form

$$Z \rightarrow aX\ldots$$
$$X \rightarrow Zx\ldots$$
$$X \rightarrow Zy\ldots$$

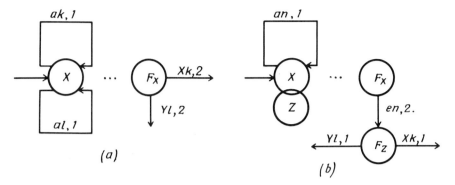

Fig. 2.27. Substitution for edges-loops in initial vertexes

Figure 2.27*b* shows the transformed graph. It fully matches the extended grammar. We pursue examining the edges. Suppose the edges are incident out of some vertex which is the end vertex X of an automaton of the system. Here we deal with the edges (F_X, Y). The vertex Y cannot be intermediate, by the state graph's construction. If Y is the initial vertex of the automaton system, then the grammar contains the productions

$$\to XaYx\ldots$$
$$\to XaYy\ldots$$

or

$$\to \ldots XaYx\ldots$$
$$\to \ldots XaXy\ldots$$

The edges labeled 1 and bearing the terminal a correspond to the first case; the second case admits the edges with arbitrary numbers. Let us transform the state graph using the above techniques for the first group of productions. The original graph and the graph transformed are shown in Figure 2.28*a* and *b*. The transformed graph matches the productions

$$Z \to XaY$$
$$\to Zx\ldots$$
$$\to Zy\ldots$$

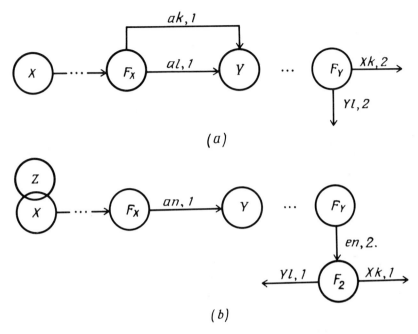

Fig. 2.28. Transforming edges (F_X, Y) labeled 1

Analogous substitution for the second group of productions yields

$$Z \rightarrow XaY$$
$$\rightarrow \ldots Zx \ldots$$
$$\rightarrow \ldots Zy \ldots$$

The original and transformed graphs are shown in Fig. 2.29a and b. The transformation is analogous to the one described above. The transformed graph corresponds to the second group of productions after making substitutions in productions. The latter makes sense for $i \neq j$ and $i = 1$ or $j = 1$. The transformations cause the edge numbers, which are greater than i and j for the paths k and l, to decrease by one.

Let us examine the edges-loops (F_X, F_X) in the end vertexes of the automatons loaded with the same terminals (e.g., a). The group of productions matching these edges may be

$$X \rightarrow \ldots Xa$$
$$X \rightarrow Xa$$

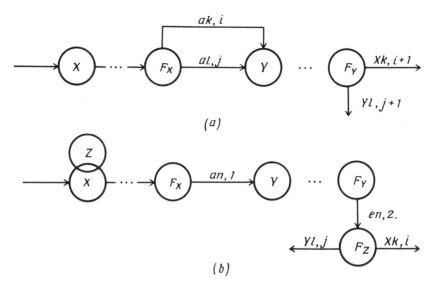

Fig. 2.29. Transforming edges (F_X, Y) numbered arbitrarily

Hence the right-hand parts of productions always end with the terminal a and the number of characters in the right-hand parts of the productions $X \rightarrow \ldots Xa$ varies. Let us consider the variant when the group contains a production of the form $X \rightarrow Xa$. Figure 2.30a shows a fragment matching the given pair of productions. Introducing a new production

$$Z \rightarrow Xa$$
$$X \rightarrow \ldots Z$$
$$X \rightarrow Z$$

we get a different state graph of Fig. 2.30b where the edges-loops have been replaced with the edges (F_Z, F_X) bearing empty strings. The selection of these edges is also ambiguous when parsing. Therefore using this transformation is inexpedient. We adjourn the discussion of the case.

A careful look at Fig. 2.30b reveals that the case, where the edges (F_Z, F_X) are loaded with empty strings, has not yet been considered. Increasing their loads can help us make parsing deterministic (see Figs. 2.22 and 2.24). The state graph (Fig. 2.30b), after transformation, will take the form shown in Fig. 2.30c.

We pursue considering the edges which link the end vertexes. Examine two

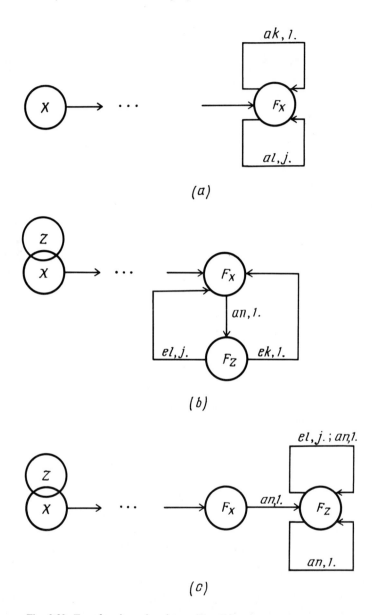

Fig. 2.30. Transforming edges-loops (F_X, F_X)

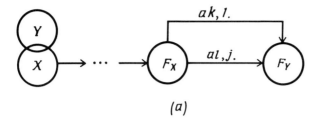

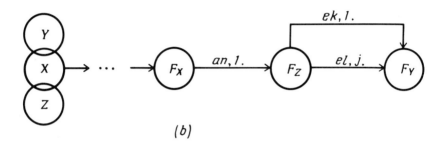

Fig. 2.31. Transformating edges (F_X, F_Y) for X-Y

edges (F_X, F_Y) each loaded with the terminal a. The appropriate grammar fragment is

$$Y \to Xa$$
$$Y \to \ldots Xa$$

The state graph is shown in Fig. 2.31a

$$Z \to Xa$$
$$Y \to Z$$
$$Y \to \ldots Z$$

The transformed graph has also the edges (F_Z, F_Y) whose selection is ambiguous. This ambiguity can be removed by applying the techniques given above. We outline the transformation process for the edges $(F_X; F_Y)$. In transforming the edges (F_X, F_Y), we introduce a new vertex F_Z and the sole edge (F_X, F_Z) labeled 1 and bearing the terminal a. The edges (F_Z, F_Y) substituted for (F_X, F_Y) have the same loads except for the terminal a replaced with a space character. Note that the given transformation is valid for the edges (F_X, F_X) as well.

Let us talk about general principles of separating the edges in view of increasing their loads. For the edge (X, Y) with the load am, k the load-increasing process can be pictured as follows. Each edge (Y, Z) with load xp, i is supplied by the new edge (X, Z) loaded into $am, k; xp, i$ for (a) $m = p$ and $k = i - 1$ and (b) $m \neq p, i = 1$ or k-edge is the last edge of the path m. On passing into the state Y along the edge loaded into am, k, parsing can only be continued for the edges which comply with the above conditions. The edge (X, Y) is then deleted. If no edge is incident into the vertex Y, it should be deleted as well. Figure 2.32 illustrates the transformation. It is immaterial for the given transformation whether initial, intermediate, or end vertexes are involved.

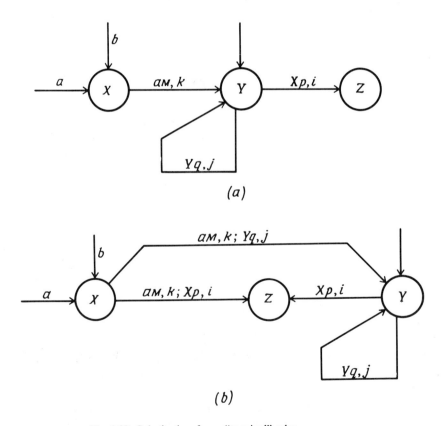

Fig. 2.32. Substitution for a "terminal" edge

Transforming Edges-Loops

The edges-loops, if present in initial or end vertexes of the automaton system, cause a lot of trouble in separating edges. Let us examine the edge (X, X) loaded into am, 1, where X is an initial vertex of the automaton system. Note that the edge with the terminal a in the vertex X is unique. If there exist more such edges, then the transformation can be performed in accord with Fig. 2.27. Suppose the node X admits a sole edge $(X, \ldots)$ with the terminal a. This case requires no transformations, because parsing is unambiguous. If there is at least one more such edge, the loads of other edges $(X, \ldots)$ should be increased on the left (Fig. 2.33). Thus, the edge (X, Y) is supplied with one more edge (X, Y), and its load bp, 1; $\ldots$ is complemented with am, 1, on the left. This is valid for initial nodes $(i = 1)$. Such an increase of the loads is not necessary for all the edges. For instance, we deal with the edge (X, Z) which bears the terminal a, and $Z \neq X$. Increasing the load on the right results

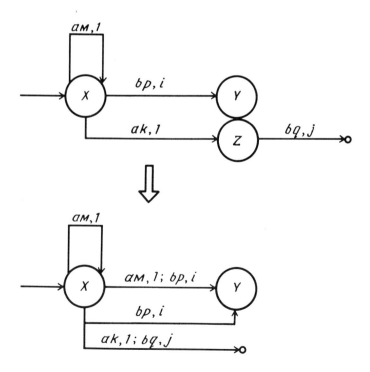

Fig. 2.33. Transforming "terminal" edges in initial vertexes of the graph

in adding bq, j to ak, 1. Hence the edges $(X, \ldots)$ loaded into bp, 1; ... will only need increasing their loads on the left.

Now let us consider the edges having their complex loads increased on the right, which cannot be selected unambiguously. Their transformations can give rise to edges-loops with complex loads. Consider them in much the same way. Figures 2.34 and 2.35 illustrate an example of such a load and operation on it in fragments. First, the loads of the edges bearing the terminal a are separated and then the loads, with the terminal b. Finally, all the edges $(X, \ldots)$ differ from each other. If the edges are arranged in decreasing order of their loads, the first edge available for transition will provide unambiguous parsing.

Let us revert to the consideration of edges-loops located in the end vertexes of the system automatons (Fig. 2.36). The main difficulty resides in ordering these edges. Separation of edges by increasing the loads on edges (F_X, C) $(C \neq F_X)$ is time-consuming because a great number of edges will have to be introduced. Recollect the forms of grammar productions, which give rise to the edges-loops in end vertexes,

$$X \to Xa$$
$$X \to \ldots Xa$$

If the input tape contains some current character a, then transition along one of these edges will result in termination of parsing the appropriate production. Let us consider the case when the stack contains the number of path l, i.e. parsing has begun in accord with the l-th production. Otherwise, the transition along the edge (F_X, F_X) of path l cannot be performed for $j \neq 1$.

If the stack content is consistent with routing the edge of the path l, this causes the substitution $X \to \ldots Xa$ to be completed. Starting from the current character, two characters a present on the input tape can cause the following replacement of configurations:

$$(F_X, aaw, l.s, j - 1.q') \vdash (F_X, aw, s, q')$$
$$\vdash (F_X, w, s', q'')$$

for $a \in T$, $w' \in T^*$, $s = l.s'$, $q' = j - 1.q''$, and

$$(F_X, aaw, l.s, j - 1.q') \vdash (F_X, aw, s, q')$$
$$\vdash (F_X, w, s, q')$$

for $a \in T$, $w' \in T^*$, $s \neq l.s'$.

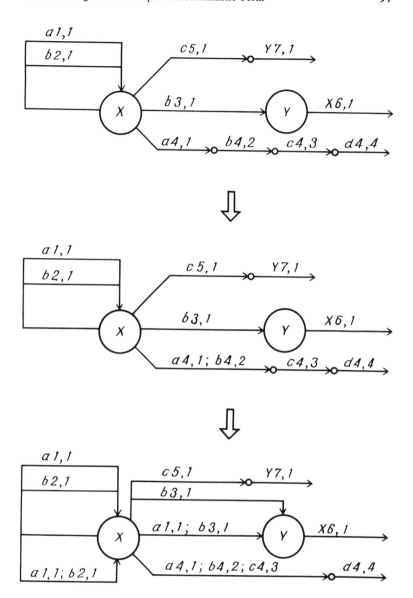

Fig. 2.34. Edges-loops in initial vertexes in view of complex loads

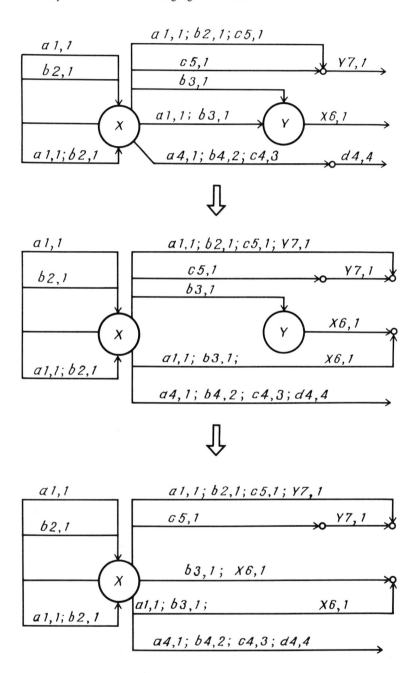

Fig. 2.35. Edges-loops in initial vertexes in view of complex loads (cont. from Fig. 2.34)

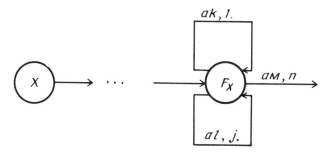

Fig. 2.36. Edges-loops in end vertexes

The productions were arranged as follows:

$$X \rightarrow \ldots Xa$$
$$X \rightarrow \ldots Xa$$

or

$$X \rightarrow \ldots Xa$$
$$X \rightarrow Xa$$

The change of configurations below admits two characters aa:

$$(F_X, aaw, l.s, j - 1.q') \vdash (F_X, aw, l.s, j - 1.q')$$
$$\vdash (F_X, w, s, q')$$

This matches parsing the productions

$$X \rightarrow Xa$$
$$X \rightarrow \ldots Xa$$

Thus, if the input tape contains more than one character a including the current one, the final configuration does not depend upon the order of parsing the given productions. The presence of one character a demands that parsing be completed along the path l. Hence the edges (F_X, F_X) can be arranged in the following order. If the edge held in the stack has the number more than 1, then this edge should be analyzed first.

The edges $(F_X, \ldots)$ are separated as is the case with the edges-loops in initial nodes. At each step of transformation examined the pair of edges $(Fx, \ldots)$, (Fx, Fx) for $j \neq 1$, proceeds to the edges $(Fx, \ldots)$, (Fx, Fx) for $j = 1$ (Fig. 2.36). Increasing the loads of the edges on the left is independent of their numbers. Such edges placed in initial nodes should be first numbered. Consider some grammars to illustrate the above transformations.

Examples of Graph Transformations

Shown in Fig. 2.19 is the state graph of the LL (2)-grammar whose productions are

$$S \rightarrow dAs \mid AbS \mid e$$
$$A \rightarrow cbA \mid d$$

Two edges, (S, S) and (A, F_A), labeled 1 and loaded into the terminal d leave the vertex S. Increasing the load of the edge (A, F_A) (see Fig. 2.32) makes the selection of the edges unambiguous in accord with the transformations suggested. Three edges, i.e. two (F_A, S) and one (F_A, F_A), are incident out of the vertex F_A. That is why the edge (S, F_A) will be replaced with two edges (S, S) and one edge (A, F_A) (Fig. 2.37a). Let us analyze whether the selection of edges loaded with

$$d5, 1.; \ b2, 1 \text{ and } d5, 1.; \ e1, 2 \text{ or}$$
$$d5, 1.; \ b2, 1 \text{ and } d5, 1.; \ e4, 3$$

is ambiguous, when the stack contains the numbers of both paths and edges, i.e. 1, 1 and 4, 2, and the input tape holds the characters db. Because, no edges bearing the first terminal b, rise from the vertex S, all the edges $(S, \ldots)$ can be placed in the following order:

edge (S, S) loaded with $d5, 1.; \ b2, 1$

edge (S, S) loaded with $d5, 1.; \ e1, 2$

edge (S, F_A) loaded with $d5, 1.; \ e4, 3$

The edge loaded with 4, 1 can be disposed at any place up to the "empty" edges. The priority of the empty edges (S, F_S) loaded with $e1, 3.$ and $e2, 2 \ldots$ is minimal. These edges will remain empty, for they enter the end vertex of the initial automaton of the system.

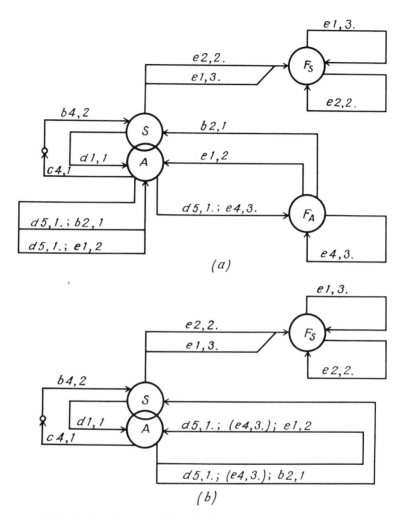

Fig. 2.37. Transforming a graph for *LL* (2)-grammar

Such an arrangement of edges and the presence of the characters *db* on the input tape ensure routing the edge loaded with *d*5, 1.; *b*2, 1., because the latter will be met with first in selecting the edge available for the transition from the vertex *S*. Thus we have ordered the edges to be selected in the vertex *S* except for the one loaded with *d*1, 1. Routing this edge and *d*5, 1.; *e*4, 3. and *d*5.1.; *e*1, 2.is equiprobable in the presence of the character *d* on the input tape. One can easily check to see that further increasing the loads of edges will not solve the problem, the reason being the presence of the edge-loop (F_A, F_A).

Let us resume examining the original state graph (see Fig. 2.19). Routing the edge (S, F_A) once performed, initiates either one or several transitions along (F_A, F_A) or causes no transitions along this edge at all. Let $(e4, 3.)$ denote the infinite set of sequences separated by a colon, i.e. {space: $e4, 3.: e4, 3.: e4, 3.: e4, 3.; e4, 3.; e4, 3.: \ldots$}. The elements of the set represent the record of some complex load of the edges which consists of one load element $e4, 3$. Routing the edge (A, B) loaded with $(e4, 3.)$, the change of configurations

$$(A, a, SS', qq') \vdash (B, a, SS', qq')$$

takes place if $S = 4$ or $q = 2$, or else the configuration

$$(A, a, SS', qq') \vdash (A, a, SS', qq')$$

recurs for $S = 4$ and $q = 2$.

Taking account of all the above-stated, increase the load on the edge (A, F_A) (see Fig. 2.19) to two instead of three edges (S, S) (Fig. 2.37b) loaded as follows:

$$d5, 1.; (e4, 3.); e1, 2$$
$$d5, 1.; (e4, 3.); b2, 1$$

Here the transition along the edge (F_A, F_A) has a priority over the transition along the edge (F_A, S) loaded with $b2, 1$ (see Fig. 2.19). As already mentioned, routing the edge-loop is performed first if the edge $(F_A, \ldots)$ labeled 1 of path n does not match some final edge $(\ldots, F_A)$ of the same path. The path labeled 2 which contains the edge (F_A, S) loaded with $b2, 1$ tends towards the vertex F_S but not F_A. This validates increasing the load of the edge (Fig. 2.37b).

Examine the graph shown in Fig. 2.37b. The priorities of the edges (S, S) loaded with $d1, 1$ and $d5, 1.; (e4, 3.); e1, 2.$ are the only point at issue. On going along these edges the state does not change. If the transition along an edge caused the stack content to decrease, then this edge will have higher priority of the two available for transition. Thus the edge loaded with $d5, 1.; (e4.3.); e1, 2$ will precede the one loaded with $d1, 1$.

Let us return to the source grammar corresponding to the state graph shown in Fig. 2.19.

$$S \rightarrow dAS \mid AbS \mid e$$
$$A \rightarrow ebA \mid d$$

An empty edge once introduced to separate the vertexes S and A matches the productions

$$S \rightarrow dAS \mid eAbS \mid e$$

Then the original state graph takes on the form shown in Fig. 2.38a. The path (A, A) consists of two edges loaded with $c4$, 1; $b4$, 2. Introduce a notation as is the case with the empty edges-loops, i.e. ($c4$, 1; $b4$, 2). On going along such a route or the edge (A, B) either no operations are performed or the following change in configurations recurs, if possible,

$$(A, cbw, s', q') \quad \vdash (A, bw, 4.s', 1.q')$$
$$(A, bw, 4.s', 1.q') \; \vdash (A, w, 4.s', 2.q')$$

The change in configurations iterates for $w = cbw'$, etc.

Increase the loads on edges (S, A) and (S, F_S) (Fig. 2.38a). In the first case, two edges (S, S) with the following load (Fig. 2.38b):

$$d1, 1; (c4, 1; b4, 2); d5, 1.; (e4, 3.); e1, 2$$
$$e2, 1; (c4, 1; b4, 2); d5, 1.; (e4, 3.); b2, 2$$

are obtained. These edges differ by their terminal loads. The former is loaded with the terminals dd and the latter with db.

Let us transform the state graph (see Fig. 2.20) of the LR (2)-grammar with the productions

$$S \rightarrow A, S \mid A$$
$$A \rightarrow aB$$
$$B \rightarrow b \mid b, B$$

Delete empty edges following the adopted procedure. The graph considered has an empty edge (F_B, F_A) loaded with $e3$, 2. . Increase its load on the right. This will give an edge (F_B, S) loaded with $e3$, 2.;, 1, 1 and a path (F_B, F_S) loaded with $e3$, 2.; $e1$, 2. (Fig. 2.39a). The vertex F_A can be deleted and the path (F_B, F_S) becomes an edge. The two edges leaving the vertex B are loaded

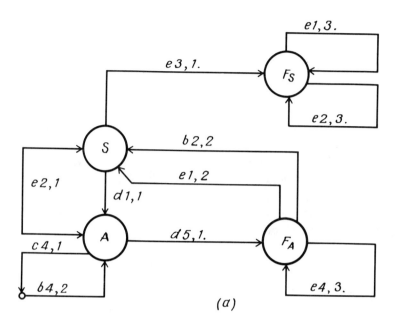

(a)

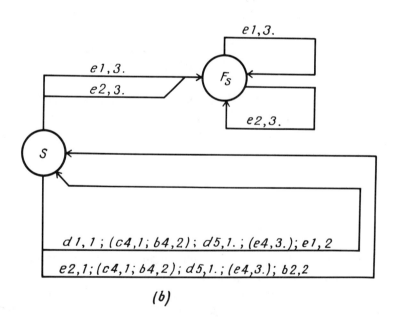

(b)

Fig. 2.38. Transforming a graph for LL (2)-grammar, initial vertexes isolated

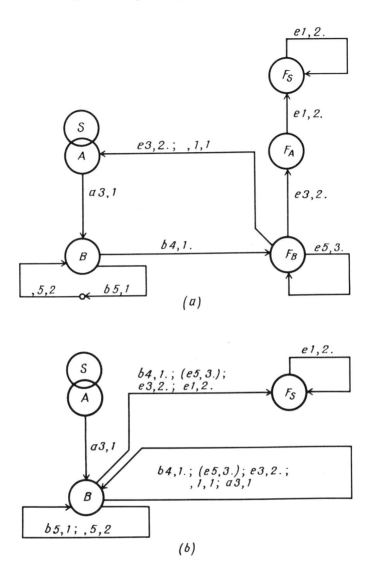

Fig. 2.39. Transforming a graph for *LR* (2)-grammar

with identical terminals b. Hence, three edges bearing complex loads will rise from the vertex B (Fig. 2.39b). Arrange the loads in descending order according to their priorities,

$b4$, 1.; ($e5$, 3.); $e3$, 2.;, 1, 1; $a3$, 1

$b5$, 1.;, 5, 2

$b4$, 1.; ($e5$, 3.); $e3$, 2.; $e1$, 2.

Note that the edge-loop (B, B) cannot be expressed in the form of ($b5$, 1;, 5, 2), for the edge (B, F_B) is loaded with the character b and can be followed by the edge (F_B, A), their loads separated by a comma.

So, we have discussed two examples for different types of context-free grammars. Using the transformations suggested we have reduced the state graphs to their deterministic form. In the course of transformations we had proposed an abbreviated form to record the loads of the edges-loops.

Now let us examine the grammar matching the indeterministic automaton constructed in Chapter 1. Its productions are

$S \rightarrow E$

$E \rightarrow T \mid E + T \mid E - T$

$T \rightarrow F \mid T * F \mid T/F$

$F \rightarrow a \mid b \mid c \mid (E)$

Figure 2.40 shows the state graph of this grammar. Each of the vertexes F_T and F_F, has three edges loaded with a space character e. Consider the vertex F_T. All the edges enter one and the same end vertex F_E and are loaded respectively with $e6$, 1., $e7$, 2. and $e8$, 2. They complete one of three substitutions in accord with the rule $E \rightarrow T \mid E + T \mid E - T$. The alternative, what edge, $e7$, 2. or $e8$, 2. to choose, can be resolved depending on the path opened in the stack before. No path is opened, the transition is performed along the edge of path six. Thus, the edges can be arranged as $e7$, 2., $e8$, 2., $e6$, 1 or $e8$, 2., $e7$, 2., $e6$, 1.. The edges (F_F, F_T) can be handled similarly. Thus, the given state graph can be used for parsing sentences of a language, without making any additional transformations.

However, each of the vertexes, F_T or F_F, can have at least one edge rising from it, i.e. (F_T, X) and (F_F, Y) for $X \neq F_E$ and $Y \neq F_T$. In more complicated cases it is necessary to delete the empty edges. Note that three edges enter the vertex F_E and four edges leave it. Using conventional techniques, we shall

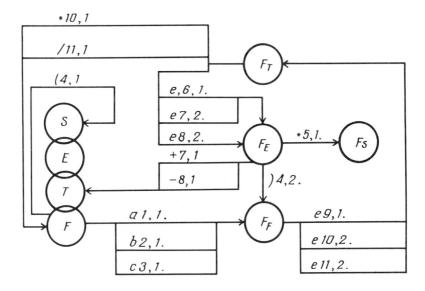

Fig. 2.40. State graph for algebraic expression grammar

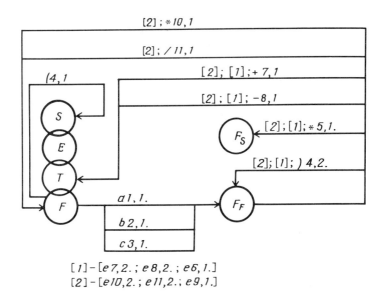

Fig. 2.41. Transformed state graph for algebraic expression grammar

introduce twelve ($3 \times 4 = 12$) edges (F_T, ...) and arrange them according to their priorities. Deleting the newly created vertex F_T will permit us to arrange 42 edges by their priorities (3 edges enter and 14 edges leave the vertex).

To simplify such transformations, let us introduce the ordered set [$n1$; $n2$; $n3$; ...] for the groups of the edges (A, B) which leave one and the same vertex A and enter the same vertex B. Notice that their loads are arranged in accord with their priorities, i.e. $n1$, $n2$, $n3$, ... Substitute the only edge (A, B) loaded with the set introduced for the group of edges (A, B). The transition along the edge is considered possible if the change of configurations matching the load n can take place. Searching for loads does not upset their order. Substitute one edge loaded with [$e7$, 2.; $e8$, 2.; $e6$, 1.] for the edge (F_T, F_E) and that with the load [$e10$, 2.; $e11$, 2.; $e9$, 1.] for the edge (F_F, F_T).

After merging the edges (F_T, F_E) and (F_F, F_T), increase their loads on the right till the terminals appear to get the state graph of Fig. 2.41. Note that the number of edges decreased simultaneously with increasing the loads.

Consider another example often met with in grammars. The grammar fragment is

$$A \rightarrow aBc \mid aCd$$
$$B \rightarrow bAd \mid c$$
$$C \rightarrow bAx \mid d$$

Figure 2.42a shows the state graph for the given grammar. Increasing the loads of the edges (A, B) and (A, C) produces the graph of a new form shown in Fig. 2.42b. Now we have got two edges-loops (A, A) with identical terminal loads. Let us reduce them as is the case with the edges-loops having ordinary loads. Introduce a new route n. The only edge loaded with an, 1.; bn, 2. will replace the edges (A, A). Connect the vertex F_A with a new vertex F_Z by the edge bearing en, 3. . Both first and second initial edges-loops ended respectively with edge 1 of path 3 and edge 1 of path 5. Therefore, remove their extensions to the vertex F_Z to obtain the edges (F_Z, F_C) and (F_Z, F_B) (Fig. 2.42c). Now the edges of the state graph can be selected unambiguously. The loads of the edges (F_Z, F_B) and (F_Z, F_C) can be obviously reduced. We can write $e1$, 1; $e3$, 1. for $e1$, 1; $e3$, 1; $d3$, 2. and $e2$, 1; $x5$, 1... for $e2$, 1; $e5$, 1; $x5$, 2. .

Reducing the edges-loops with their ordinary loads we have never transferred the load onto the outgoing edges (see Fig. 2.27). Such a transfer, when performed, causes the loads ek, 1; xk, 2 and el, 1; yl, 2 to be assigned to the edges (F_Z, ...). This load can be rewritten in the form xk, 1 and yl, 1 if all the edge numbers of paths k and l are decreased by one. This was mentioned in examining the graph shown in Fig. 2.27a.

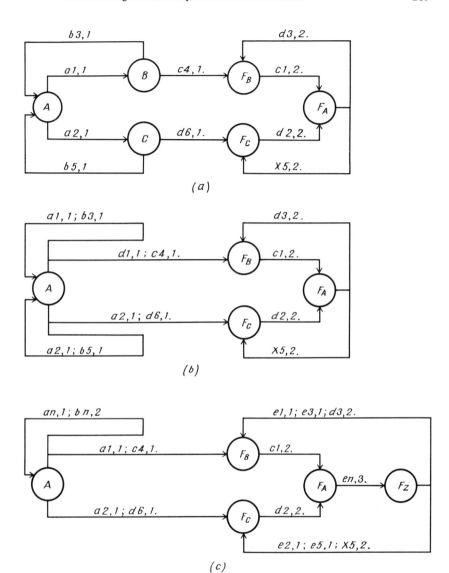

Fig. 2.42. Fragment of state graph

Thus, we have discussed various examples. Nearly all of them deal with indeterministic state graphs. Using the suggested techniques, all the graphs were reduced to their deterministic form. At the same time simplified expressions for writing the loads of edges and their groups were introduced.

The technique applied for reducing the state graphs to their deterministic form affected the structure of the graphs without causing any change in the type of language. A number of transformations were illustrated with the appropriate equivalent changes of the grammars. If searching of equivalent grammars was not obvious, transformations were performed such that for every vertex all the paths available for parsing suffered no changes.

The present chapter analyzed context-free languages. For going over from grammars to automaton systems certain restrictions were imposed on their types. The state graph of the automaton system for simple grammars required no additional transformations to become deterministic. The traditional techniques could not always provide deterministic parsing for some grammars not modified beforehand. These state graphs were reduced to their deterministic form as well. More complicated grammars were supplied with deterministic state graphs after performing the suggested transformations and all the possible fragments of the state graphs were analyzed. Hereinafter the algorithms of transformations will be considered in detail.

3 Parsing Formal Languages in Multiprocessor Systems

3.1. Parsing Context-Sensitive Languages

The previous chapter dealt with context-free languages and discussed parsing them by means of the reduced state graph of the automaton system. The present chapter examines whether the state graph is usable for parsing context-sensitive languages. The type of the state graph is determined in the same way as in the previous chapter.

According to the definition, no restrictions of the form

$$v \in (T \cup N)^* \times N \times (T \cup N)^*, \; w \in (T \cup N)^*$$

are imposed on the productions $v \to w$ of the context-sensitive grammar $G = (N, T, P, S)$ of type $\emptyset$.

Let us divide all the productions into groups [11]. Each group comprises the productions containing one and the same nonterminal N_i in their left-hand parts, i.e. $P: L_j N_i R_j \to u^i_{j,1}, u^i_{j,2}, \ldots$. The number of productions in groups varies for every nonterminal. Both left- and right-hand contexts determine whether the nonterminal N_i can be replaced. A single group of productions is put in correspondence with each nonterminal. Figure 3.1 presents the orient-

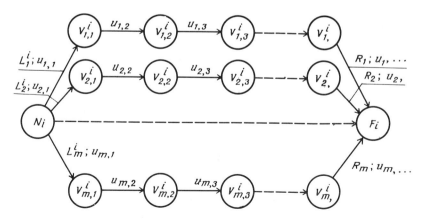

Fig. 3.1. State graph for an automaton matching context-sensitive grammar

ed loaded graph for the group assigned to the nonterminal N_i. The state graph is constructed similarly to the graph of context-free languages except for initial and terminal edges loaded with left- and right-hand contexts, respectively. If $L_j, R_j = e$ for all the paths j, the state graph will turn into one of the context-free languages. The given graph can be considered as transition graph for the general case of a indeterministic automation.

Let us represent the automaton A_i by the quintuple

$$(Q_i, \; T_i \cup Q', \; t_i, \; q_{0i}, \; F_i)$$

where Q_i = nonempty set of states

$\qquad T_i$ = set of input terminals

$\qquad q_{0i} \in Q_i$ = initial state

$\qquad F_i \in Q_i$ = terminal state

$$Q' = \bigcup_{i=1}^{n} \{ \text{lab } (q_{0i}) \}$$

$\qquad$ lab (y) = labeling function

The labeling function sets up a correspondence between each state and its label,

$$\text{lab } (y) = (y = q_{0i} \rightarrow \, 'q_{0i}', \; y \in T \rightarrow y, \; y = e \rightarrow e)$$

Henceforth, we shall denote as the nonterminal the initial state of the appropriate automaton, the label of the initial state, and the nonterminal. The transition function is specified by the following expression:

$$t_i : Q_i \times (T_i \cup Q') \times Z_i \rightarrow R(Q_i) \qquad\qquad (3.1)$$

where $R(Q_i)$ = set of all the subsets of the states Q

$$Z_i = \bigcup_{j=1}^{m} \{ L_j, R_j \} = \text{set of contexts}$$

Expression (3.1) sets a certain relationship between the change of states and both the current content of the input tape and parsing the source sentence from its beginning up to the current character registered in some special manner. The left-hand context helps tentative routing in the initial state N_i, the right-hand one validates the route selected for the transition to the final state. For lack of context expression (3.1) changes into a form similar to that of the automaton corresponding to context-free languages.

Let us collect the automatons N_i into the system $\{N_1, N_2, \ldots, N_n\}$, where N_1 is the initial automaton which corresponds to the initial grammar character S, $N_1 = S$. Introduce the sets

$$Q = \bigcup_{i=1}^{n} Q_i, \ T = \bigcup_{i=1}^{n} T_i, \ Z = \bigcup_{i=1}^{n} Z_i$$

Since $Q_i \cap Q_k = \varnothing$ for $i \neq k$, we can rewrite the transition function:

$$t : Q \times (T \cup Q') \times Z \rightarrow R(Q) \tag{3.2}$$

Note that for lack of context we also revert to the automaton system matching context-free languages examined earlier. Therefore, we expect the system properties to remain unchanged except for passing the initial and terminal edges of the paths.

Identification corresponds to the transition along the edges of the automaton state graph from the initial state N_1 to the terminal state F_1. Let us introduce two stacks to register the context on both initial and terminal edges. The first stack is intended to register parsing entirely from its start up to the current character on the input tape. This stack helps to reveal which left-hand context assigned to the initial edges of the paths has been saved in stack in some current state while parsing. The second stack contains the right-hand context for further parsing. By the end of parsing the first stack holds all the series of productions applied in parsing; the second stack should be empty.

The first stack (denoted ML) is a string of terminal, nonterminal and special characters $\{[,]\}$. Thus, its alphabet is a set $T \cup N \cup \{[,]\}$. The stack is filled in from left to right in identifying the source sentence. Before parsing starts, the stack is kept empty, i.e. $ML = e$. Suppose $ML = y$ and the transition takes place along the edge (A, B). If A is the initial state of the automaton system, then $ML = y \ [A;$ and $ML = y] \ D$ for the final state B (e.g. $B = F_D$). The transition along the edge loaded with some terminal a requires that the latter should be put down in the stack on its right, i.e. $ML = ya$. Passing the edge, which bears either a space character or a nonterminal, has no effect on the stack content. Transformations performed on the state graph deprive the edge of the nonterminal load. Thus the stack *ML* registers the whole parsing process.

The content of the stack *ML* is examined to see whether the transition along the edge bearing the left-hand context is possible. The transition can be performed if the context has been registered while parsing. To compare the stack string and the context, replace the context nonterminals N_i with the groups of characters $N_i[\ ]N_i$. Comparison takes place in initial vertexes of the state graph. The context and the stack string are compared from right to left.

Let the context $x_1 x_2 ... x_n$ be compared with the stack string $ML = = y_1 y_2 ... y_m$. The comparison algorithm is as follows:

1. Specify initial values $i = n > 0$ and $j = m > 0$.
2. Compare x_i with y_j. If $x_i \neq y_j$, then use step 5. For $x_{i-1} x_i =]N_k$, compute $i = i - 2$ and decreasing j by 1 till $y_{j-1} y_j \neq N_k[$. While decreasing, count the characters $]N_k$ met with. If the number of such characters is equal to m, then search for the $(m + 1)$-st pair of the characters $N_k[$ by decreasing j concurrently. Then use the next step.
3. Compute $i = i - 1$, $j = j - 1$.
4. If $i \neq 0$ and $j \neq 0$, use step 2. If $i = 0$, terminate comparing and infere that the right-hand substring of the stack corresponds to the given context. If $j = 0$, $i > 0$, there is no appropriate right-hand substring in the stack for the given context.
5. If $x_i \in T$ and $y_j \in \{N, [,]\}$, compute $j = j - 1$ and use step 4. If $x_i \in N$, $x_{i-1} =]$, $y_j \in \{[\} \cup N$, then compute $j = j - 2$ and go to step 2. If $x_i \in N$, $x_{i-1} =]$, $y_j \in T$, there is no right-hand substring in the stack for the given context.

Let us consider an example. Some context can be isolated from the stack

$$ML = S\ [abcA\ [x]AB[A\ [yzkd]\ Ad]\ B, \text{ i.e. } B = B[\ ]B;\ d;$$

$$A[\ ]Ad;\ kdd;\ xB[\ ]B;\ xA[\ ]A, \text{ etc.}$$

The second stack (denoted by *MR*) is a set of strings $MR = \bigcup_{k=1}^{l} MR_k$, where l is the number of contexts of the set *MR*. Each string of the set is an expected right-hand context. Filling the set *MR* takes place during transitions along the edges loaded with some right-hand context. In routing the edge the context R_j complements the set *MR*, i.e. $MR = MR \cup R_j$.

The stack *MR* is used for additional routing verification of the state graph upon parsing. As in the left-hand context, the nonterminals N_i of the right-hand context are represented as strings $N_i[\ ]N_i$. Let us see how additional verification is carried out and wether the terminal load of the edge corresponds to the context expected. The stack consists of strings of the form $x_1 x_2 ... x_n$, where $x_i \in T \cup N \cup \{[,]\}$. Each string of the set MR is subjected to the same manipulations. The leftmost character of each string should be analyzed.

Suppose there is some string of the form xw, $w \in (T \cup N \cup \{[,]\})^*$. The transition is effected along the edge (A, B). If A is the initial vertex of the automaton system and $x = A$, the string $xw = A[w'$ is deprived of all the characters $A[$, on the left. Otherwise the string will remain unchanged. Let $a \in T \cup \{e\}$ be the load of the edge. For $a = e$ the string content does not change and transition can be executed. When $a \neq e$, $x \in T$ and $x \neq a$ the transition along the edge (A, B) is not admissible, for it is not consistent with the context expected. The character x can be either terminal or nonterminal, or]. When $a \neq e$ and $x \in N$ the transition along the edge is not admissible, for it does not conform to the anticipated context. For $x =]$, transition along the edge is possible and the given string of the set MR suffers no changes. The vertex B is considered last. If B is the terminal vertex of some automaton of the system, then to go along it the leftmost characters $] B$ of the set MR, if present, should be deleted from the string $xw =]Bw'$.

Let us re-define the transition function to make it correspond to the state graph,

$$t(v, \ u_{j,1}, \ L_j) = \{v_{j,1}\} \tag{3.3}$$

if $v \in N$ and the context L_j can be extracted as a right-hand substring of the string ML or $L_j = e$.

$$t(v, \ u_j, \ \ldots, \ R_j) = \{f\} \tag{3.4}$$

where f is a terminal state of an automaton of the system. The following three expressions describe transition along the edges without taking account of contexts. They are identical to the record of the transition function for automaton system matching context-free languages.

$$t(v, \ u) = \{u\} \tag{3.5}$$

for $u \in N$;

$$t(F_y, \ e) = \{v_{j,l}\} \tag{3.6}$$

where F_y is a terminal state of the automaton $Y \in N$ and there exists the edge $(v_{j,l-1}, v_{j,l})$ loaded with the nonterminal $u_{j,l} = Y$, and the transition to the state Y from the state $v_{j,l-1}$ is performed last.

$$t(v_{j,l}, u) = \{ v_{j,l+1} \} \tag{3.7}$$

where $u \in T \cup \{e\}$ is identical to the current character on the input tape. The last condition must be satisfied for the transitions complying with expressions (3.3) and (3.4).

When use is made of expressions (3.3), (3.4) and (3.7) check to see whether the transition taking place and the expected context of the set MR are consistent with each other. No such check is required if the set MR is empty ($MR = \varnothing$) and no restrictions are imposed on the expected context. The transition performed in accord with expression (3.3) causes modification of stacks (i.e. the sets ML and MR). On using (3.4) the set MR is complemented, as stated in defining the stacks. Thus, parsing context-sensitive and context-free languages differ in checking the transition for compliance with the right-hand context; recording the parsing process in the string ML; and in modifying the stacks.

Suppose that at all steps of the process of the given several paths of identification, a correct path is chosen, and the state graph is indeterministic in the general case. Then the language $L(G)$ and the one admitted by the system of automatons become identical. Parsing terminates on scanning the source sentence on the input tape, when $MR = \varnothing$ and the state F_1 is current. If it is not possible to leave the current state, the source sentence is not considered admissible and does not belong to the examined language. By the end of parsing, the string ML holds a procedure of applying rules for parsing the source sentence.

To ascertain the form of expressions for the transition function, let us perform three transformations on the state graph in much the same way as for context-free languages. These transformations are almost similar except for some corrections when account is taken of both left- and right-hand contexts.

1. Introduce complementary edges, each loaded with an empty string e. Such edges do not change the grammar form. Finally the user is interested not in the number of space characters in the source sentence of the language but in the sentence considered as a sequence of terminals. Moreover, the space characters of the source sentence are implicit. For passing the empty edges of the graph no manipulations are performed on the source string.

Introduce the complementary edge $(v_{j,l}, v_{j,k})$ with $u_{j,k} = e$ for $u_{j,l}$,

$u_{j,l+1} \in Q'$; $v_{j,l} = F_i$. The load of the edge introduced can be appended by the right-hand context R_j assigned, if present, to the edge $(v_{j,l-1}, v_{j,l+1})$. Thus, we get the following sequence of states: $\{\ldots, v_{j,l}, v_{j,k}, v_{j,l+1}\}$. The left-hand context L_j, if it exists, can be removed onto the edge newly created for $l = 1$, i.e. $u_{j,l} \in Q'$. The present transformation is equivalent to the space characters introduced into the right-hand parts of grammar productions and placed either between the adjacent nonterminals or after the rightmost nonterminal of the production.

Note that a space character should precede the nonterminal located at the beginning of a nonleft-recursive production. Thus the left-hand context, if present, can be loaded onto the first empty edge. Left-recursive productions do not allow the empty string to be inserted, and the context locates on the next, terminal or empty edge.

2. Let both numbers of the route proceeding from the initial vertex N_i to the end vertex F_i and the ordinal edge number of the route be applied to every edge loaded with either terminal or empty character $(u_{j,l} \in T \cup \{e\})$. Numbering should avoid identical pairs of numbers. Thus, $(s, q)^i_{j,l} = (s, q)^k_{j',l'}$ is only valid for $i = k$, $l = l'$, $j = j'$. Two stacks M and D store the current information concerning parsing.

3. Because we have taken the context from the edges loaded with nonterminals onto the newly introduced edges, the latter can be deleted only after performing the following transformation. Let us examine the edge $(v_{j,l}, v_{j,l+1})$ loaded with the nonterminal N_i. The state $v_{j,l}$ and the initial state N_i merge for $u_{j,l+1} = 'N_i'$. The terminal state of the edge integrates with the terminal state of the automaton A_i. When the given transformation is performed for all the "nonterminal" edges the transition specified by expressions (3.5) and (3.6) are realized.

The state graph now consists of edges which bear terminal and space characters combined with left- and right-hand contexts. Routing these edges proceeds in agreement with expressions (3.3), (3.4) and (3.7) of the transition function. Let us represent these expressions in the form of configuration change of the control unit.

For the system of automatons matching context-sensitive languages the control unit configuration is represented not by the quadruple but by the sextet of parameters. The first four elements of configuration are identical to those of context-free languages. The first element is the current state; the second element is a part of the input string from the current character and up to the end. The third and fourth elements represent the current states of the stacks M and D which contain respectively the numbers of paths and edges.

The fifth element stores the whole parsing history from the beginning of the sentence up to the current character on the input tape. This element is the stack ML. The sixth element is the stack MR containing a set of contexts expected at the current instant of parsing. While recording the expected contexts are set off from each other by points. That is why we shall not use points in examining grammars. The last two elements of the configuration will be used strictly in correspondence with the above algorithms.

Let us describe the operations performed in passing the edge (A, B) which bears numbers (s, q) and is loaded with the nonterminal a

$$(A, \, ax, \, ss', \, nq', \, l', \, rr') \vdash (B, \, x, \, ss', \, qq', \, l', \, a, \, r') \qquad (3.8)$$

if the edge bears no context, and $a \in T \cup \{e\}$; $n = q - 1$, $x \in T^* \cup \{e\}$, $q \neq q_{max}$, where q_{max} is the maximal edge number of route s; $l', r', r'' \in (T \cup, N \cup \{[,]\})^* \cup \{e\}$; $r = a$ or $r = e$ and $r' =]r''$.

$$(A, \, ax, \, ss', \, nq', \, l', \, rr') \vdash (B, \, x, \, s', \, q', \, l'a]A, \, r') \qquad (3.9)$$

for $q = q_{max}$; $r \in \{a, \,]A,\}$ or $r = e$, and $r' =]r''$; $B = F_A$.

$$(A, \, ax, \, s', \, q', \, l', \, rr') \vdash (B, \, x, \, ss', \, qq', \, l'A[a, \, r') \qquad (3.10)$$

when $q = 1$; A is a starting vertex of the automaton, $r \in \{a, \, A[\}$ or $r = e$ and $r' =]r''$. If A is the end vertex of the automaton, e.g. $A = F_C$, then the group of characters C[is placed in the stack ML next to the one first met with on scanning from the right to the left. Passing the only edge of the path does not affect the content of the stacks M and D. Expressions (3.8) through (3.10) differ from (2.5) through (2.7) only in processing the stacks ML and MR.

Building the state graph implies that the context can be located on first or last edge of the route. Therefore, rewrite expressions (3.9) and (3.10) by taking account of both left- and right-hand contexts L and R placed on the edge (A, B).

$$(A, \, ax, \, s', \, q', \, l', \, rr') \vdash (B, \, x, \, ss', \, qq', \, l'A[a, \, r') \qquad (3.11)$$

if $q = 1$; A is an initial vertex of the automaton $r \in \{a, \, A[\}$ or $r = e$ and $r' =]r''$; the left-hand context L is a right substring of the stack ML in accord with the above algorithm. If A is an end vertex, e.g. $A = F_C$, then analysis intended to reveal whether the left-hand context can be considered a right-hand substring of the stack *ML*, should start with the characters preceding the rightmost group of characters *C*[.

$$(A, ax, ss', nq', l', rr') \vdash (B, x, s', q', l'a]A, r' \cdot R) \quad (3.12)$$

for $q = q_{max}$; $r \in \{a,]A,\}$ or $r = e$, and $r' =]r''$.

Thus the transition function is represented by expressions (3.8) through (3.12) specifying the change of configurations for the automaton system. The source string is considered admissible if all the characters of some string are consequently admitted and the string itself results from inserting a finite number of space characters into the source string. While scanning this string, the system of automatons changes from the initial configuration (S, e, e, e, e, e) into the final one (F_S, e, e, e, L, e). Here S and F_S are respectively the initial and the final states of automaton system, L is the process of parsing the source sentence registered in the stack *ML*. The language constructs admitted by the system of automatons are identical to those generated by context-sensitive grammar. As the transformations performed impose no restriction on the grammar productions, the given automaton system can be employed for parsing both context-sensitive and context-free languages.

In the general case, the state graph may be indeterministic. Reducing the graph to its deterministic form is analogous to the technique applied to context-free languages, for these graphs only differ by the complementary loads assigned to their edges, i.e. contexts. The latter not only hinder transformations but also simplify the task of reducing the graph to its deterministic form. The context is used as additional information for separating edges.

As an example consider the context-sensitive grammar

$$G = (\{S, B, P, A, B, C, D\}, \{if, begin, end, then, else,;, a, i, : =, + \}, R, S)$$

Certain traits of a programming language are inherent in this grammar. It includes both assignment and conditional statements, the identifier, and the simplified expression. The grammar productions are expressed as:

S	$\rightarrow$	begin P end
P	$\rightarrow$	$B \mid B;\ P$
B	$\rightarrow$	if A then B else B
$;B$	$\rightarrow$	$C := D$
begin B	$\rightarrow$	$C := D$
else B	$\rightarrow$	$C := D$

$$
\begin{aligned}
\text{then } B &\rightarrow & C\!:=\!D \\
A &\rightarrow & i \mid a \\
C &\rightarrow & A \mid CA \\
D &\rightarrow & C \mid C + C
\end{aligned}
$$

The nonterminal B is substituted in the dependence of the left-hand context, i.e. begin, else, then, and ;. Figure 3.2 shows the state graph constructed for the automaton system in accord with the grammar productions. The characters L: and R: followed by the context denote respectively the left- and the right-hand contexts arranged on the graph. The context is set off from the rest of load by semicolon.

Examine the edges (P, A) of the state graph. Of these, four edges bear a space character, one edge is loaded with the terminal character 'if'. The left-hand context present on the "empty" edges prompts unambiguous selection of these edges when parsing. Thus, the presence of the context makes further reducing of graphs to their deterministic forms easier. Thorough examination of the suggested graph reveals that there are edges in the vertex F_C which cannot be selected unambiguously. The graph is transformed using the technique described in the previous chapter. The reduced graph is shown in Fig. 3.3.

Figure 3.2 shows the integrated groups of vertexes, P, B and D, C, A. The edges are not strictly assigned to particular vertexes. For instance, the edge loaded with 'if' should enter the node A, but in Fig. 3.2 it is shown to enter the vertex C. This was permissible for context-free languages. However, in the present case parsing is consequently registered in the stack ML. The productions are registered by names of the initial vertexes where the transitions start. Therefore, constructing the state graph requires that all the initial vertexes of the automaton system be separated from each other (Fig. 3.3). On deleting such vertexes during transformations, the vertex name together with its load are shifted onto the new edge (Fig. 3.3).

Parsing the string

$$\text{begin if } a \text{ then } i : a \text{ else } a\!: = a + i \text{ end}$$

initiates the following sequence of the change of configurations:

$(S, \text{begin if } a \ldots , e, e, e, e \vdash (P, \text{if } a \text{ then } \ldots , 1, 1, S$
$[\text{begin}, e)$
$\vdash \quad (A, a \text{ then}..., 4.\ 1,\ 1.\ 1,\ S\ [\text{begin } P\ [B\ [\text{if}, e)$
$\vdash \quad (F_A, \text{ then}..., 4.\ 1,\ 1.\ 1,\ S\ [\text{begin } P\ [B\ [\text{if } A\ [a]\ A, e)$
$\vdash \quad (B, i : = a..., 4.\ 1,\ 2.\ 1,\ S\ [\text{begin } P\ [B\ [\text{if } A\ [a]\ A \text{ then}, e)$

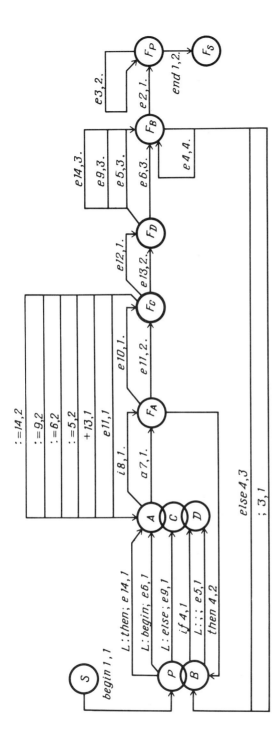

Fig. 3.2. Deterministic state graph for the automaton system matching context-sensitive grammar

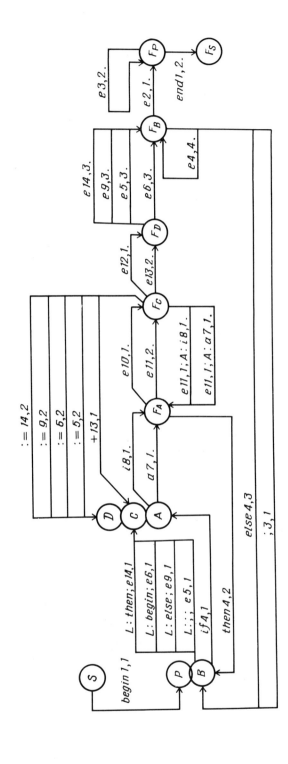

Fig. 3.3. State graph for automaton system after the arrangement of edges has been revised

⊢ $(C, i := a..., 14. 4. 1, 1. 2. 1, S$ [begin P [B [if A [a] A
   then B [, e)

⊢ $(F_A, := a..., 14. 4. 1, 1. 2. 1, S$ [begin P [B [if A [a] A
   then B [C [A [i] A, e)

⊢ $(F_C, := a..., 14. 4. 1, 1. 2. 1, S$ [begin P [B [if A [a] A
   then B [C [A [i] A] C, e)

⊢ $(D, a$ else..., 14. 4. 1, 2. 2. 1, S [begin P [B [if A [a] A
   then B [C [A [i] A] $C := $, e)

⊢ $(F_A,$ else..., 14. 4. 1, 2. 2. 1, S [begin P [B [if A [a] A
   then B [C [A [i] A] $C := D$ [C [A [a] A, e)

⊢ $(F_C,$ else..., 14. 4. 1, 2. 2. 1, S [begin P [B [if A [a] A
   then B [C [A [i] A] $C := D$[C [A [a] A] C, e)

⊢ $(F_D,$ else..., 14. 4. 1, 2. 2. 1, S [begin P [B [if A [a] A
   then B [C [A [i] A] $C := D$ [C [A [a] A] C] D, e)

⊢ $(F_B,$ else..., 4. 1, 2. 1, S [begin P [B [if A [a] A then
   B [C [A [i] A] $C := D$ [C [A [a] A] C] D] B, e)

⊢ $(B, a := a + i..., 4. 1, 3. 1, S$ [begin P [B [if A [a] A
   then B [C [A [i] A] $C := D$ [C [A [a] A] C] D]
   B else, e)

⊢ $(C, a := a + i..., 9. 4. 1, 1. 3. 1, S$ [begin P [B [if A [a]
   A then B [C [A [i] A] $C := D$ [C [A [a] A] C]
   D] B else B [, e)

⊢ $(F_A, := a + i..., 9. 4. 1, 1. 3. 1, S$ [begin P [B [if A [a]
   A then B [C [A [i] A] $C := D$ [C [A [a] A] C]
   D] B else B [C [A [a] A, e)

⊢ $(F_C, := a + i..., 9. 4. 1, 1. 3. 1, S$ [begin P [B [if A [a]
   A then B [C [A [i] A] $C := D$ [C [A [a] A] C]
   D] B else B [C [A [a] A] C, e)

⊢ $(D, a + i..., 9. 4. 1, 2. 3. 1, S$ [begin P [B [if A [a] A
   then B [C [A [i] A] $C := D$ [C [A [a] A] C] D]
   B else B [C [A [a] A] $C := $, e)

⊢ $(F_A, + i..., 9. 4. 1, 2. 3. 1, S$ [begin P [B [if A [a] A
   then B [C [A [i] A] $C := D$ [C [A [a] A] C] D]
   B else B [C [A [a] A] $C := D$ [C [A [a] A, e)

⊢ $(F_C, + i..., 9. 4. 1, 2. 3. 1, S$ [begin P [B [if A [a] A
   then B [C [A [i] A] $C := D$ [C [A [a] A] C] D]
   B else B [C [A [a] A] $C := D$ [C [A [a] A] C, e)

⊢ $(C,$ iend, 13. 9. 4. 1, 1. 2. 3. 1, S [begin P [B [if A [a]
   A then B [C [A [i] A] $C := D$ [C [A [a] A] C]

D] B else B [C [A [a] A] C := D [C [A [a] A] C
+, e)

⊢ (F_A, end, 13. 9. 4. 1, 1. 2. 3. 1, S [begin P [B [if A [a]
A then B [C [A [i] A] C := D [C [A [a] A] C]
D] B else B [C [A [a] A] C := D [C [A [a] A] C
+ C [A [i] A, e)

⊢ (F_C, end, 13. 9. 4. 1, 1. 2. 3. 1, S [begin P [B [if A [a]
A then B [C [A [i] A] C := D [C [A [a] A] C]
D] B else B [C [A [a] A] C := D [C [A [a] A] C
+ C [A [i] A] C, e)

⊢ (F_D, end, 9. 4. 1, 2. 3. 1, S [begin P [B [if A [a] A then
B [C [A [i] A] C := D [C [A [a] A] C] D] B else
B [C [A [a] A] C := D [C [A [a] A] C + C [A
[i] A] C] D, e)

⊢ (F_B, end, 4. 1, 3. 1, S [begin P [B [if A [a] A then
B [C [A [i] A] C := D [C [A [a] A] C] D] B else
B [C [A [a] A] C := D [C [A [a] A] C + C [A
[i] A] C] D] B, e)

⊢ (F_B, end, 1, 1, S [begin P [B [if A [a] A then
B [C [A [i] A] C := D [C [A [a] A] C] D] B else
B [C [A [a] A] C := D[C [A [a] A] C + C [A
[i] A] C] D] B] B, e)

⊢ (F_P, end, 1, 1, S [begin P [B [if A [a] A then
B [C [A [i] A] C := D [C [A [a] A] C] D] B else
B [C [A [a] A] C := D[C [A [a] A] C + C [A
[i] A] C] D] B] B] P, e)

⊢ (F_S, e, e, e, S [begin P [B [if A [a] A then
B [C [A [i] A] C := D [C [A [a] A] C] D] B else
B [C [A [a] A] C := D[C [A [a] A] C + C [A
[i] A] C] D] B] B] P end] S, e)

The considered source string belongs to the language generated by context-sensitive grammar. The stack *ML* contains the whole sequence of the grammar productions applied in parsing. Other stacks are empty. The automaton system is in its final state. Thus the suggested approach can be considered applicable to parsing both context-free and contest-sensitive languages. At a later stage, the operation algorithms will be given in more detail.

A case has been examined where parsing is the only process. Of essential interest is the possibility of implementing state graphs in multiprocessor mode of parsing the original sentences of languages.

3.2.   Parallel Computer Systems and Processes

Discussing the above techniques of parsing both context-free and context-sensitive languages, we have not touched upon their applicability to parallel processing of sentences of a language. Let us overview the basic types of parallel computing systems.

Serial computer takes turns in fetching instructions and data from its memory, executes the instructions and stores the results. Both instruction and data streams support the interface between the memory and the central processor. Thus an ordinary computer associates with one instruction stream and the only data stream. Overlapping the operations is inherent to a certain extent in all the present-day computers. Various functional units can be involved in parallel processing arithmetic operations, different processors can concurrently operate on several tasks or parts of the same task. Such outperforming systems are employed at EDP centers to increase their capacities. Among them are multiprocessing systems which handle k tasks using p processors and m memory blocks. Parallel computer systems fall into these systems as well, for they involve p processors to execute a task. Thus multiprocessing systems admit operation on several data and instruction streams.

The software design for parallel computer systems requires that special technological facilities be developed to support concurrent calculations. The parallel programming techniques are based on two multiprocessing strategies, synchronous and asynchronous [8]. In compliance with *synchronous strategy*, the computing sequence is subdivided into steps. Each step involves a series of operations (Fig. 3.4)

$$A_i = [A_{i,1}, A_{i,2}, \ldots, A_{i,l}]$$

applied at a time to large data arrays

$$\{v_{i,1}, v_{i,2}, \ldots, v_{i,m}\}, i = 1, 2, \ldots, n$$

In the *asynchronous mode*, several computing branches are processed simultaneously (Fig. 3.5). Waiting processes and interchanges between parallel branches w_i need special interface channels.

Pipeline multiprocessing occupies an important place among multiprogramming trends. It involves simultaneous application of the arranged sequence of various instructions P_i to the data stream $v_1, v_2, \ldots, v_m$ (Fig. 3.6). The data handled by P_i are subjected to the instruction P_{i+1}. Mul-

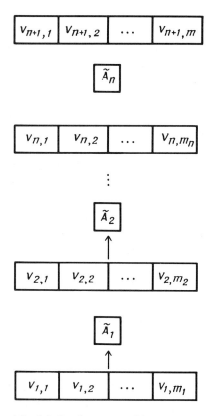

Fig. 3.4. Synchronous multiprocessing

tiprocessing systems are instructions realized as components of either hardware or software. Let us consider in more detail the former component.

We would like to highlight three traits being the most essential for multimodular systems [12].

1. Multiprocessing involves modules or processors not available beforehand for their number; the main memory communicates to each module at two access levels: rapid-access internal memory and add-in memory located in other modules and additional units.

2. Realignment of communications should be possible between elementary machines, i.e. transputers, able to store, handle and transfer data.

3. Multimodular systems, though having identical communications protocols, data formats, base instructions set of the processors (elementary

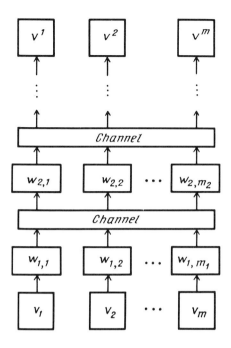

Fig. 3.5. Asynchronous multiprocessing

machines), can differ to some extent by memory capacity, number of coprocessors, etc.

These properties can variously be realized for different multimodular systems and affect the number of both instruction and data streams. In view of the above stated, computer systems are subdivided into four classes [13]: uniprocessor systems, parallel processors, pipelining processors, and multiprocessor computing systems (Fig. 3.7). Of great interest are multiprocessor computing systems having homogeneous structure (Fig. 3.8). Multitransputer systems can be considered as their current implementation.

By a *multitransputer system* we shall mean a modular multiprocessor which consists of transputers [12]. The latter is implemented in VLSI-chip and can store, transfer, and process data. Besides processor components, the transputer includes a memory block, a timer and an interface to supply data interchanges in the overlapping mode. Sequential channels between other transputers and peripherals are separated from memory interface, which enables joining to off-chip memory.

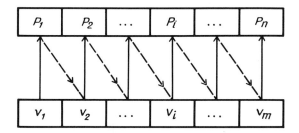

Fig. 3.6. Pipeline multiprocessing

Depending on the partitioning memory, processors, input and output units, programs and microcodes, the multiprocessor computing systems (MPCS) are divided into static and dynamic models [8]. Partitioning in *static MPCSs* suffers no changes throughout the computing process. In *dynamic MPCSs*, the partitions can vary during multiprocessing. Later on we will consider a multitransputer system as a model managing data and supporting parallel programs.

Let us treat a *parallel program* as a sequence of programs which interact and can be realized at a time. All the operations using common memory $D = \{d_i, i \in I\}$ to solve some problem result from the execution of the instruction set

$$S = \{S_k, \ k \in K\}, \ S_k \colon \bar{D} \to \bar{D}, \ \bar{D} = : \bar{d_i}$$

		Data stream	
		Single	Multiple
Instruction stream	Single	Uniprocessor system	Parallel processor and associative processor
	Multiple	Data flow processor (pipeline system)	Multiprocessor or multicomputer system

Fig. 3.7. Classification of basic types of computing system architecture

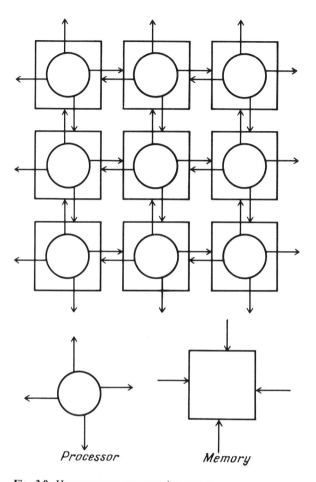

Fig. 3.8. Homogeneous computation structure

where K, I and $\bar{d}_i$ are respectively the finite sets k, i and d_i. Sequential algorithm consists of series of instructions which begin with the start instruction. Performing sequential algorithm can involve one transputer. At each time instant, its instruction register holds the name of an instruction being performed. The list of successors contains only one element, i.e. the name of the next instruction. In parallel computings several instructions can be carried out at a time. Therefore series of transputers are required to hold the names of the instructions being performed in their instruction registers. To each register there corresponds its own list of successors. The instruction once executed has its name replaced in the instruction register with its successor's name. Since this moment on a new operator starts and the list of successors opens for a new element. The successor is determined from the results of executing either the instruction assigned to the given instruction register or several instructions corresponding to other registers.

Parallel algorithm [12] which employs the memory D is defined by the quadruple (S, S', H, C) where S is a finite set of instructions over D; S' is a subset of start instructions ($S' \in S$, and each name is assigned to its own instruction register from the set H); H is a set of initial transputers, where every instruction register belongs to MPCSs. Their number should not be less than the number of start instructions. C is a set of instructions for processor interaction. Each instruction of the set C can (i) activate new transputers or halt the operating transputers; and (ii) assign a successor at any instruction register which is active at the time of executing the instruction. The set of control instructions includes the half instruction. Parallel algorithm terminates, when the last of active transputers stops.

We have discussed the basis of multiprocessing. The sequential parsing of sentences for various languages is discussed in previous sections. Here we shall examine the possibility of creating a parallel parsing algorithm for an appropriate MPCS.

3.3.   Going from Language Processor to Multiprocessor

With character multiprocessing are classed the processes occurring during concurrent translating, editing, and other types of operating on source codes. Suppose the source sentence can be divided into separate strings, each associated with its own calculation branch, which parses it on characters. This parallel calculating, if possible, is called *static multiprocessing*. As far as dynamic character multiprocessing is concerned, the source sentence is divided into strings in due course of parsing. The given section deals with static character multiprocessing, for it is the most simple and sufficiently promotes parsing.

Let us remind you of parsing which takes place in accord with the state graph. The state graph contains the information concerning the grammar of a sentence of the source language. The input and output streams are respectively the source sentence saved on the input tape with the pointer indicating the current character and the contents of four stacks, which hold route numbers, edge numbers, the productions parsed and the right contexts expected. The statements of the transition function, which cause the configurations to be changed, can be considered as the finite set of instructions applied to the input stream. The statements of the transition function rigorously comply with the information assigned to the edges of the state graph. The edges leaving each vertex undergo the examination till the one available for parsing will be found out. The same operations are applied to each edge — these are the expressions of the transition function initiating the configuration change. Thus processing each current character can concur with the analysis of the edges rising from some current vertex of the state graph.

See Fig. 3.9 for the structure of multitransputer computing system intended for parallel translating the sole source sentence. It includes n transputers to analyze edges, a control transputer, and a transputer to perform semantic operations. For a better insight into MPCS' operating we'll have to clarify the structure of records of the state graph.

The state graph can be represented by some set of vertex addresses with the initial vertex address marked out. The entire information concerning the edges is stored at the appropriate vertex addresses in consistence with their arrangement in the state graph. Every edge is associated with the address which holds the information about the edge, its load, and the address of the vertex, where the given edge enters. Semantic operations which take place while pass-

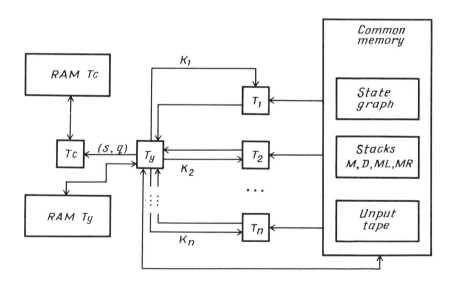

Fig. 3.9. Diagram for parallel processing the edges of system state graph

ing the edge are identified by a pair of numbers (s, q) assigned to the edge, and are represented by the program fragments written in some programming language.

So far as the information on the state graph is necessary for majority of the transputers, it is placed in common memory. The stacks and the source sentence taken from the input tape are located there as well. The transputers involved in analysis of the operations on the edge call for source information K_i, i.e. the edge address held in common memory and the value of the pointer which indicates the current character of the source sentence. Each of n transputers examines whether the transition along the edge corresponding to given address can take place. If the transition is possible, the control transputer T_y receives the address of the vertex, where enters the edge being analyzed. The response on availability of the transition will be generated, if the change of configurations can take place in accord with an expression of the transitive function. The number of transputers, i.e. n, is equal to the maximal number of edges rising from the same vertex.

Having accepted either one or several affirmative answers, the control computer selects the one corresponding with the number of the transputer. The edges of the state graph are arranged in such an order that the first affirmative answer, which results from their consequent analysis, will be true. That is why the answer selected will always come from the transputer having minimal number. After the answer has been ascertained, passing the edge examined by this transputer can be performed. In due course of passing, the address of the next vertex of the state graph is determined, the change of configurations causes the stacks be updated, the indicator shifts to the next current character. The pair of route and edge numbers is sent to the transputer T_y. Then the vertex address helps to ascertain the addresses of the edges rising from this vertex, and the information obtained is again sent to the transputers for further analysis of the edges.

Using edge numbers, the transputer T_y determines the address of semantic operations assigned to the edge and executes them. Computing lasts until the final configuration is reached.

We have discussed concurrent translation of the sole sentence. However, the source code can be represented by the set of statements. In this case several sentences of the language can be handled at the same time. Fig. 3.10 shows a structure of such a system. Each statement is parsed using the multiprocessor computing system considered above (Fig. 3.9). Such MPCSs promote creating more powerful computing systems.

To co-ordinate the activities of the base MPCS included into the new sys-

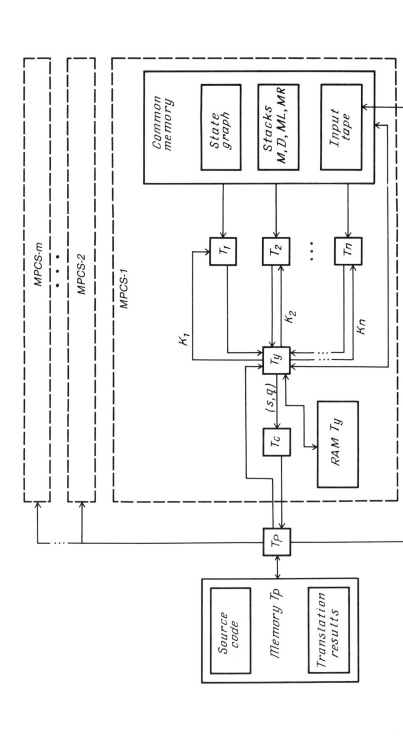

Fig. 3.10. Diagram for parallel translating sentences of a language

tem, let us complement its structure with the transputer T_p. The source program is located in the memory of this very transputer as well as the results of translation. The source sentences are removed from the memory to the base MPCS to whose control transputers the start instructions are sent. On processing the next source sentence, MPCS informs the transputer T_p, which is also responsible for consequent processing the instructions.

In view of concurrent parsing, the structure proposed is rather perfect, as syntax constructs of sentences do not affect each other. In general case, the total parallel translation can take place depending on semantic interrelationship between the sentences of the language. As these properties of the languages are consistent with their exact instantiations, each particular case calls for individual consideration.

Discussing the multiprocessor computing system, we've assumed the state graph be preliminary reduced to its deterministic form. However MPCS admits using the nondeterministic graph. Contrary to the previous variant, the state graph is not only responsible for data structure management, but forms the structure for multitransputer system to proceed from. To illustrate passing over to such an MPCS and to examine its activities, let us consider $LR(2)$ grammar and the appropriate nondeterministic state graph (see Fig. 2.20).

The structure of a state graph is entirely associated with the one of MPCS. Each vertex of the graph corresponds to a transputer. Transputers are connected in much the same way as edges of a graph (Fig. 3.11). Each transputer has the common memory as well as memory of its own. The latter holds information concerning edge loads and transputer communications. The common memory saves the information on all processes active at some current instant of time. For every process its configuration is preserved, i.e. the pointer of the current character of the input tape, the states of four stacks, and the name of the transputer next to be involved in this process.

The configuration which contains the name of the initial transputer (e.g. *TS*) is loaded into the common memory, when processing starts, and the transputer is informed to turn active. The active transputer determines whether the transition is possible proceeding from the information on the edges and the system configuration held respectively in memory of its own and in the common memory. All the edges are examined consequently. The transition being possible causes the system configuration be changed. The latter is then put into the common memory with the name of that very transputer aimed by the tansition. This transputer then receives the instruction to turn active. If the transputer has been already active, the request sent to the given transputer is enqueued. Turning active, the tranputer starts processing the first configura-

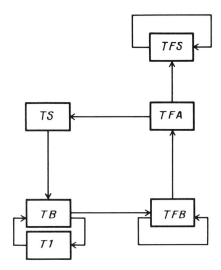

Fig. 3.11. Diagram for parallel parsing in accordance with indeterministic state graph

tion fetched from the common memory by the name of its own. Having handled all the edges matching the configuration selected, the transputer becomes passive for lack of activation demands. This makes its configuration be deleted from the common memory. The final configuration once made its appearance in the common memory causes parsing the sentence be terminated.

To avoid iterative passing the empty edges, we should reduce the state graph, i.e. delete the empty edges.

Let us look at parsing the string *ab, b, ab* for MPCS (Fig. 3.11). See Fig. 2.20 for its state graph.

> Common memory
> (TS, *ab*, *b*, *ab*, *e*, *e*, *e*, *e*)
> Transputer TS completed its task:
> Common memory
> (*TB*, *b*, *b*, *ab*, 3, 1, S [*A* [*a*, *e*)
> Transputer TB handled the edge (*B*, F_B)
> Common memory
> (*TB*, *b*, *b*, *ab*, 3, 1, S [*A* [*a*, *e*)
> (*TFB*, *b*, *ab*, 3, 1, S [*A* [*aB* [*b*] *B*, *e*)
> Transputer TB handled the edge loaded with *b*5, 1
> Transputer TFB handled the edge loaded with *e*3, 2.

Common memory
(*T*1, , *b*, *ab*, 5. 3, 1. 1, *S* [*A* [*aB* [*b*, *e*)
(*TFA*, , *b*, *ab*, *e*, *e*, *S* [*A* [*aB* [*b*] *B*] *A*, *e*)
Transputer T1 handled the edge loaded with , 5, 2
Transputer TFA handled the edge loaded with , 1, 1
Common memory
(*TFA*, , *b*, *ab*, *e*, *e*, *S* [*A* [*aB* [*b*] *B*] *A*, *e*)
(*TB*, *b*, *ab*, 5. 3, 2. 1, *S* [*A* [*aB* [*b*, , *e*)
(*TS*, *b*, *ab*, 1, 1, *S* [*A* [*aB* [*b*] *B*] *A*, , *e*)
Transputer TFA handled the edge loaded with *e*2, 1.
Transputer TB handled the edge loaded with *b*4, 1.
Transputer TS became passive
Common memory
(*TFS*, , *b*, *ab*, *e*, *e*, *S* [*A* [*aB* [*b*] *B*] *A*] *S*, *e*)
(*TB*, *b*, *ab*, 5. 3, 2. 1, *S* [*A* [*aB* [*b*, , *e*)
(*TFB*, , *ab*, 5. 3, 2. 1, *S* [*A* [*aB* [*b*, *B* [*b*] *B*, *e*)
Transputer TFS became passive
Transputer TB handled the edge loaded with *b*5, 1
Transputer TFB handled the edge loaded with *e*5, 3.
Common memory
(T1, , *ab*, 5. 5. 3, 1. 2. 1, *S* [*A* [*aB* [*b*, *B* [*b*, *e*)
TFB, , *ab*, 3, 1, *S* [*A* [*aB* [*b*, *B* [*b*] *B*] *B*, *e*)
Transputer T1 handled the edge loaded with , 5, 2
Transputer TFB handled the edge loaded with *e*3, 2.
Common memory
(TB, *ab*, 5. 5. 3, 2. 2. 1, *S* [*A* [*aB* [*b*, *B* [*b*, ,*e*)
(TFA, , *ab*, *e*, *e*, *S* [*A* [*aB* [*b*, *B* [*b*] *B*] *B*] *A*, *e*)
Transputer TB became passive
Transputer TFA handled the edge loaded with , 1, 1
Common memory
(TFA, , *ab*, *e*, *e*, *S* [*A* [*aB* [*b*, *B* [*b*] *B*] *B*] *A*, *e*)
TS, *ab*, 1, 1, *S* [*A* [*aB* [*b*, *B* [*b*] *B*] *B*] *A*, ,*e*)
Transputer TFA handled the edge loaded with *e*2, 1.
Transputer TS handled the edge loaded *a*3, 1
Common memory
(TFS, , *ab*, *e*, *e*, *S* [*A* [*aB* [*b*, *B* [*b*] *B*] *B*] *A*] *S*, *e*)
(TB, *b*, 3. 1, 1. 1, *S* [*A* [*aB* [*b*, *B* [*b*] *B*] *B*] *A*, *S* [*A* [*a*, *e*)
Transputer TFS became passive
Transputer TB handled the edge loaded with *b*4, 1.
Common memory
(TB, *b*, 3. 1, 1. 1, *S* [*A* [*aB* [*b*, *B* [*b*] *B*] *B*] *A*, *S* [*A* [*a*, *e*)
(TFB, *e*, 3. 1, 1. 1, *S* [*A* [*aB* [*b*, *B* [*b*] *B*] *B*] *A*, *S* [*A* [*aB* [*b*] *B*, *e*)
Transputer TB handled the edge loaded with *b*5, 1
Transputer TFB handled the edge loaded with *e*3, 2.
Common memory
(T1, *e*, 5. 3. 1, 1. 1. 1, *S* [*A* [*aB* [*b*, *B* [*b*] *B*] *b*] *A*, *S* [*A* [*aB* [*b*, *e*)
(TFA, *e*, 1, 1, *S* [*A* [*aB* [*b*, *B* [*b*] *B*] *B*] *A*, *S* [*A* [*aB* [*b*] *B*] *A*, *e*)

Transputer T1 became passive
Transputer TFA handled the edge loaded with $e2$, 1.
Common memory
(TFS, e, 1, 1, S [A [aB [b, B [b] B] B] A, S [A [aB [b] B] A] S,
      e)
Transputer TFS handled the edge loaded with $e1$, 2
Common memory
(TFS, e, e, e, S [A [aB [b, B [b] B] B] A, S [A [aB
[b] B] A] S] S, e)

Final Configuration

    While parsing the given string as many as three transputers were active
at the same time. Note that when parsing, the final configuration can be
achieved before all transputers have become passive except for the final one.
In this case the final configuration once reached results in their switching off.
This approach makes the time spent for parsing executed in accord with
the nondeterministic graph coincide with the time spent to process the consequent instantiation matching the deterministic state graph. Using the above
multiprocessor computing system (Fig. 3.9) instead of transputers makes parsing more fast-acting.
    Thus using the state graph for parsing the sentences of a language admits
either consequent or parallel instantiation of the process. MPSC, if applied,
enables parsing the sentences notwithstanding whether the state graph is deterministic or nondeterministic.

3.4.   Portability of Language Processors

        The possibility to implement a language processor in some
programming language is of vital interest. However automatic or semiauto-
matic translating the processor into some other programming language sufficiently expands the field of its application. By *software portability* we shall
basically mean the possibility of its automatic translating from a language
to another and respectively from one computer to another. To make software
portable, some host language and a macrogenerator [14] are advisable to be
developed.
    So far as the present book deals with computer-aided design of language
processors, we shall consider portability from this point of view. The generator

of language processors can be developed proceeding from formal grammars and the above transformations of state graphs. The next chapters suggest a version of such a generator. Having handled the language processor recorded in some higher-level language (i.e. metalanguage), the generator outputs the same processor instantiated in the programming language.

Metalanguage is a language specifying formal grammars in Backus-Naur form provided with semantic operations. The latter is connected with certain parts of grammar productions in some special way. Semantic operations can be recorded either in some programming language or in macrolanguage. In the first case the language processor generated will be realized in the programming language identical to the one applied to semantic operations. The second case will present the language processor recorded in macrolanguage. Its further translation into a programming language should be provided with macrodefinitions supplied with macroexpansions written in the desirable programming language. Thereafter language processor should be handled by the macrogenerator. Thus you can make portable the language processor generated in macrolanguage. Passing over to some other programming language requires that the macrolibrary be updated. Using the techniques suggested by the second variant ensures portability of both the generator of language processors and the appropriate macrogenerator. The same host language as applied to language processors having their semantics written in macrolanguage substantially simplifies the problem. Since both generator and macrogenerator are realized as parsers, they can be recorded in metalanguage. Thus you'll have your record simpler and shorter, so far as the metalanguage is specially intended for this purpose.

See Fig. 3.12 for the scheme of porting software developed in metalanguage from the n-th programming language into the $(n + 1)$st one. Suppose there exist

1 the generator of language processors and the special macrogenerator described in metalanguage with its semantics in recorded macrolanguage;

2 their certain instantiation in the n-th programming language;

3 some completed version of a language processor implemented in macrolanguage.

To help porting the language processor, we shall only involve a part of the scheme suggested, viz. the macrogenerator in the n-th programming language, the macrolibrary of the $(n + 1)$st language, the source text of the processor written in macrolanguage, and the $(n + 1)$st language compiler. To generate a new version of the language processor, its source text written in macrolanguage enters the macrogenerator. The latter substitutes macrocalls

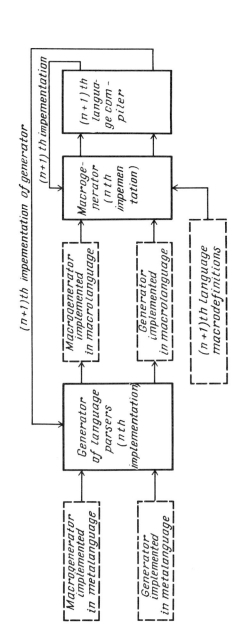

Fig. 3.12. Chart for porting parser generator from one programming language to another

in accord with macrodefinitions saved in the library. The outcoming text will be recorded in $(n + 1)$ programming language. On translating the text with a help of this language compiler (which can be located even on another computer) and its binding, we get the load module of the language processor for another computer.

Porting the generator and macrogenerator corresponds with the entire scheme shown in Fig. 3.12. Their description realized in metalanguage L_M enters the generator of n-th instantion which translates it into macrolanguage. At this time, creating the state graph, reducing it to the deterministic form and packing into the appropriate data structures of macrolanguage are taking place. Further operations are similar to those applied to porting the sole processor. Using the macroexpansions for the $(n + 1)$st programming language and the existing instantiation of macrogenerator helps translating from the n-th programming language into the $(n + 1)$st one. The translation from the $(n + 1)$st language involves its standard compiler. Having got ready-to-use programs to be substituted for the software already developed, we extend the abilities of the $(n + 1)$st language. The entire process can be repeated for the next programming language. So far as porting from one language to another implemented on some other computer is possible, porting from one computer to another can also take place.

Development of the first applicable version is the most time-consuming. Guided by the scheme assumed you can produce it using the techniques of successive approximations. Suppose we are going to change the programming language but to expand the scope of its potentialities. So first, create the version with minimal language resources. Proceeding from the version already operating, develop then the new one having more ample scope of its abilities. And on performing the whole porting cycle, you'll get the enhanced version, etc.

Thus comprehensive using the techniques suggested helps you, whenever necessary, to expand the range of their application on the basis real languages and make them portable from one computer to another. Porting causes macro-definitions, which are insufficient against the software ported, be only updated.

The present chapter completes discussing the questions on developing formal language processors, which admit parallel parsing sentences in multitransputer systems. Later on we're going to describe both a version of the generator intended for such language processors and its application.

4   Parser Description Metalanguage

Formal grammars have been used to record the original texts of the language processors. They can only be employed to describe the language syntax. On the whole, such a form matches well the generator of language processors, which are only involved in syntax analysis. However, the latter is of interest as it enables parallel processing of sentences in compliance with their meaning. That is why we need some original form which can both specify the language syntax as concisely as the formal grammars do not provide mapping of the sentence sense and the operations being performed. This chapter discusses a language variant called metalanguage, for it is intended for language description.

4.1.   Metalanguage Syntax

Metalanguage is a context-free language. Let us use the modified Backus form to describe its syntax. A group of rules (or productions) having the same nonterminal in their left-hand parts can be represented by the sole construct which consists of a nonterminal separated from the set of right-hand parts of the rules by the symbols ::=. The symbol | sets off the right-hand parts from each other. Thus the Backus-form construct is as follows:

nonterminal ::= string 1| string 2| ...

We have already used a similar record with the symbol → instead of ::= . The nonterminals represent a letter, a word or some sequence of words separated by blanks. The string is a sequence of terminals and nonterminals. Because the nonterminals imply some concepts, they are enclosed in corner brackets, i.e. ⟨and⟩. The terminals denote themselves and can constitute words. For instance,

⟨assignment statement ⟩ :: = ⟨variable identifier⟩
= ⟨expression⟩

⟨integer⟩ ::= ⟨digit⟩|⟨integer⟩⟨digit⟩
⟨digit⟩ ::= 0|1|2|3|4|5|6|7|8|9

The example includes the following nonterminals : ⟨assignment statement⟩, ⟨variable identifier⟩, ⟨expression⟩, ⟨integer⟩, ⟨digit⟩ and the terminals: = , 0, 1, 2, 3, 4, 5, 6, 7, 8, 9.

To point out that a string may be absent or recur no matter how many times, it should be enclosed in two-character corner brackets ⟨∗ and ∗⟩. Thus,

⟨integer⟩ ::= ⟨digit⟩ ⟨∗digit∗⟩

denotes the infinite string of the form

⟨integer⟩ ::= ⟨digit⟩|⟨digit⟩⟨digit⟩|
                ⟨digit⟩ ⟨digit⟩⟨digit⟩|
                ⟨digit⟩ ⟨digit⟩⟨digit⟩⟨digit⟩|...

To point out an optional string, i.e. the string which can be absent, use square brackets. For instance,

⟨loop statement⟩ ::= [⟨simple loop name⟩]
                      [⟨iteration rule⟩]
                      ⟨main loop⟩
                      [⟨simple loop name⟩]

The given construct shows that it is not obligatory to include the simple loop name and the iteration rule into the record of the loop statement. The main loop must always be present.

The metalanguage intended to describe language processors is a combination of language syntax recorded in the form of some formal grammar and language semantics realized as sentences of a programming language. Thus, the language processor comprises a series of formal grammar productions including the statements of a programming language. All the productions which contain one and the same nonterminal in their left-hand parts are grouped. As metalanguage is a context-free language, let us describe its syntax using the above-stated form.

⟨metalanguage⟩ ::= [/∗⟨comment⟩∗/]⟨production group⟩
                    ⟨∗production group∗⟩

⟨production group⟩ ::= ⟨nonterminal⟩ : ⟨production⟩
            ⟨ * production * ⟩
⟨production⟩ ::= [/ * ⟨comment⟩ * /] # [L: ⟨context⟩ E]
            ⟨element⟩⟨ * element * ⟩
            [R: ⟨context⟩ E]
⟨element⟩ ::= ⟨predicate⟩[/ * ⟨comment⟩ * /]
            [⟨semantics⟩][/ * ⟨comment⟩ * /]
            [//⟨diagnostics⟩//][/ * ⟨comment⟩ * /]
⟨semantics⟩ ::= N: ⟨identifier⟩ | P: ⟨semantic
            character⟩⟨ * semantic character * ⟩
⟨predicate⟩ ::= '⟨term chain⟩' | «nonterminal»
            [⟨number⟩]| *
⟨number⟩ ::= ⟨digit⟩[⟨digit⟩]
⟨term chain⟩ ::= ⟨term⟩⟨ * term * ⟩
⟨nonterminal⟩ ::= ⟨character⟩⟨ * character * ⟩
⟨comment⟩ ::= ⟨comment character⟩⟨ * comment
            character * ⟩
⟨diagnostics⟩ ::= ⟨diagnostic character⟩⟨ * diagnostic
            character * ⟩
⟨identifier⟩ ::= ⟨semantic character⟩ ⟨ * semantic
            character * ⟩
⟨term⟩ ::= ⟨character⟩|⟩|/| * |#
⟨comment character⟩ ::= ⟨character⟩|⟩|/|'|#
⟨diagnostic character⟩ ::= ⟨character⟩|⟩| * |'|#
⟨semantic character⟩ ::= ⟨character⟩|⟩|/| * |'
⟨context⟩ ::= «nonterminal»|'⟨term chain⟩'|
            ⟨context⟩«nonterminal»|
            ⟨context⟩'⟨term chain⟩'
⟨character⟩ ::= A| B| C| D| E| F| G| H| I| J| K| L|
            M| N| O| P| Q| R| S| T| U| V| W| X| Y|
            Z| a| b| c| d| e| f| g| h| i| j| k| l| m| n| o|
            p| q| r| s| t| u| v| w| x| y| z| .| ,| "| :| @|
            &| !| ?| -| ;| ⟨| (|)| —| +| [|]| {| }| 0| 1|
            2| 3| 4| 5| 6| 7| 8| 9
⟨digit⟩ ::= 0| 1| 2| 3| 4| 5| 6| 7| 8| 9

The syntax of semantics is defined by the syntax of an algorithmic language used in its records. That is why the programming language change-over can result in the modification of the above metalanguage syntax. This causes the interpretation to be altered for the nonterminals ⟨character⟩, ⟨semantic character⟩, ⟨comment character⟩, ⟨diagnostic character⟩. The control characters may also be revised.

The grammar makes it obvious that the space character is replaced with the * symbol when recording a predicate in the metalanguage. The predicate is an obligatory part of the ⟨element⟩ contrary to ⟨semantics⟩, ⟨diagnostics⟩, and ⟨comment⟩. Blanks can be inserted at any place in metalanguage; this enables arranging the text of the language processor convenient for examination. It is recommended that new productions, predicates, and diagnostics should be put down from the first position and semantics, from the fifth one. See Appendix 1 for the present metalanguage recorded using its own means. The next section deals with the assignment of every metalanguage construct.

4.2.   Description of Metalanguage Instructions

As follows from the above-stated syntax, the description of the language processor in metalanguage comprises a series of production groups. Each production group begins with the nonterminal identical to that of formal grammar which was inherent in every left-hand part of the productions of the given group. Let us examine the formal grammar of a decimal number. Its productions represented in the Backus form are

⟨decimal⟩ ::= ⟨number⟩ . ⟨number⟩ ;| ⟨number⟩;
⟨number⟩ ::= ⟨digit⟩|⟨number⟩⟨digit⟩
⟨digit⟩   ::= 0| 1| 2| 3| 4| 5| 6| 7| 8| 9

The given example shows three groups of productions. The first two groups contain two productions each, the third group consists of ten productions. In compliance with metalanguage these groups should begin with their names, i.e. decimal, number, digit. Each production is put down separately. The beginning of each production is marked with the # symbol which can be considered at the same time as end of the previous production. The # character and the name of the production group taken together set off the groups from one another. For instance,

decimal # ...
number # ...
digit # ...

The characters "number #" inform that the record of the production group "decimal" has come to an end and that of the production group "number" has started. The production consists of some sequence of elements limited on both sides by contexts if the grammar contains them. There are no contexts in the above grammar.

The element is either a comment or a sequence of three components, i.e. predicate, semantics and diagnostics. Each of them can be followed by some comment. The predicate is an obligatory component. In the absence of semantics, only syntax is specified. Diagnostics, if present only concerns the production given and is printed if parsing has begun but has not been completed because of some error in the source sentence.

The predicate is specified using a dummy character *, nonterminal or a term chain which is the string of terminals. The number assigned to the predicate points out how many substitutions of the present nonterminal take place in the production. The * character is analogous to the empty string *e*. Let us record the above example in metalanguage.

> decimal # ⟨number⟩ ' · ' ⟨number⟩ '; ' # ⟨number⟩ '; '
> number # ⟨digit⟩ # ⟨number⟩⟨digit⟩
> digit # '0' # '1' # '2' # '3' # '4' # '5' # '6' # '7'
>   # '8' # '9'

The given example does not contain semantics, hence the language processor discussed will only perform parsing. To make this example more complicated assume that the number contains no more than five digits both before and after the decimal point. Then the production group is

> number # ⟨digit⟩ # ⟨number⟩ [4] ⟨digit⟩

The production # ⟨number⟩⟨digit⟩ allows the nonterminal ⟨number⟩ be substituted no more than four times: # ⟨number⟩⟨digit⟩ three times; and ⟨digit⟩ once. Thus we have got a five-digit number:

> ⟨number⟩⟨digit⟩ → ⟨number⟩⟨digit⟩⟨digit⟩
>   → ⟨number⟩⟨digit⟩⟨digit⟩⟨digit⟩
>   → ⟨number⟩⟨digit⟩⟨digit⟩⟨digit⟩⟨digit⟩
>   → ⟨digit⟩⟨digit⟩⟨digit⟩⟨digit⟩⟨digit⟩

Let us show how to apply comments and diagnostics in the present example.

```
decimal
/ * parsing decimal number * /
#  ⟨number⟩
' . '
⟨number⟩
' ; '  //the sentence is not a decimal number//
#  ⟨number⟩
' ; '  //the sentence is not a decimal number//
number / * parsing five-digit number * /
#  ⟨digit⟩
#  ⟨number⟩ 4 ⟨digit⟩
//the number contains more than 5 digits//
digit / * parsing digits * /
# '0'  # '1'  # '2'  # '3'  # '4'  # '5'  # '6'
# '7'  # '8'  # '9'
```

The program given contains comments to clarify the assignment of each production group. Two production groups include diagnostics. While processing, the parser issues a message that the source sentence contains some error. The type of the error message depends on the group of productions that caused parsing to be terminated.

Using semantic operations, we can make the given program not only perform parsing but pack the number into a variable. The metalanguage allows semantics to be recorded in two ways. Semantics beginning with the characters *N*: imply that the mark of a program fragment stands next, the characters *P*: are immediately followed by the program fragment itself. The program fragment can be performed if the production element including semantics has been involved in parsing a current character of the source sentence. As already mentioned, semantics should be recorded in some programming language in accord with the language processor generator. The suggested version employs Pascal. Having complemented the processor by semantic operations, we obtain the following program composed in metalanguage (chislo is the Russian for number and cifra is the Russian for digit):

```
decimal
/ * parsing decimal number * /
#  ⟨number⟩
' . '
          P:DCHS := CHISLO;
```

⟨number⟩
';'
P:FOR I:=1 to NUMBER DO
CHISLO := CHISLO/ 10;
DCHS := DCHS + CHISLO;
//the sentence is not a decimal number//
⟨number⟩
';'
          P:DCHS := CHISLO;
//the sentence is not a decimal number//
number / *parsing five-digit number */
⟨digit⟩
          P: CHISLO := CIFRA;
          NUMBER := 1;
⟨number⟩ 4
⟨digit⟩
          P: CHISLO := CHISLO * 10 + CIFRA;
          NUMBER := NUMBER + 1;
//number is of more than five digits//
digit / *parsing digits */
'0'
          P:CIFRA := 0;
'1'
          P:CIFRA := 1;
'2'
          P: CIFRA := 2;
'3'
          P: CIFRA := 3;
'4'
          P:CIFRA := 4;
'5'
          P:CIFRA := 5;
'6'
          P: CIFRA := 6;
'7'
          P:CIFRA := 7;
'8'
          P: CIFRA := 8;
'9'
          P: CIFRA := 9;

Variable specifications are usually placed in a separate program fragment and can be included into the first fragment of the program recorded in metalanguage. The given program includes the following variable specifications.

> VAR
>> I, NUMBER : INTEGER;
>> CIFRA, CHISLO, DCHS: REAL

As follows from the program, the result of computations, i.e. a real number, is assigned to the variable DCHS. The variable CIFRA saves the value of each digit analyzed. The value of the first digit of the number is assigned to the number being generated and the digit counter of NUMBER is set into 1. Further parsing of digits results in both adding their values to the previous value of the number multiplied by 10 and increasing the counter by one. The latter helps to extract the fractional part of the number CHISLO if it contains the decimal point.

The grammar discussed is context-free and does not illustrate the arrangement of contexts in metalanguage program. The context-sensitive grammar was examined in the previous chapter. Let us compose a parser in metalanguage for it.

```
S # 'begin' ⟨P⟩ ' end'
//source sentence contains an error//
P # ⟨B⟩
  # ⟨B⟩'; ' ⟨P⟩
B # 'if' ⟨A⟩ 'then' ⟨B⟩ 'else' ⟨B⟩
  # L: 'begin' E⟨C⟩':= ' ⟨D⟩
  # L: 'else' E⟨C⟩' := ' ⟨D⟩
  # L: 'then' E⟨C⟩' := ' ⟨D⟩
  # L: ';' E⟨C⟩' := ' ⟨D⟩
A # 'i' # 'a'
C # ⟨A⟩ # ⟨C⟩ ⟨A⟩
D # ⟨C⟩ # ⟨C⟩' + '⟨C⟩
```

The example only deals with the left context placed at the very beginning of the production.

The above examples have covered almost all the metalanguage constructs. Specifying semantics is most tedious. It requires binding of semantic operations with the elements of productions. Nevertheless, one can notice some regularities which are covered in the following section.

4.3. Metalanguage Programming Techniques

The development of a language processor can be subdivided into two separate stages. The first stage covers description of the formal grammar of the language processor in metalanguage and its debugging. Main difficulties are faced in developing a language and an appropriate formal grammar. It is much easier to translate the formal grammar into metalanguage because without semantics it hardly differs from the grammar proper. Recording syntax of the expected language processor requires that the main attention should be paid to arrangement of diagnostics.

The second stage introduces semantic operations bearing the language meaning inscribed into a metalanguage program. To arrange them correctly one should realize the process of parsing performed in accord with the state graph, and understand some regularities of transforming productions into the state graph. This knowledge is not necessary for the user. Therefore, we shall clarify these regularities, proceeding from the formal grammar productions. The state graphs will be involved only for additional explanations. Let us discuss the design of a language processor in steps.

Formal grammar is designed routinely because the means suggested are not intended to automate the process. It is expedient to record the productions of the grammar being developed in metalanguage to avoid the need of translating it from one language to another.

Diagnostics' arrangement. Diagnostic messages inform a user of an error which has taken place when parsing. The above scheme suggested for parsing according to the state graph helps not only to reveal the error accurate to a character of the source sentence but to point out the productions inconsistent with the current character of a sentence. This information can be used for automatic correction of errors.

The type of syntax error can easily be related to the production which caused termination of parsing. Therefore, metalanguage diagnostics is assigned to the production, i.e. lack of correspondence between the current character and the element of the production can be commented upon in the diagnostic text of this production recorded in the metalanguage in creating the grammar.

Let us discuss the possibility of introducing diagnostics into the above program written in metalanguage. What diagnostics could be inserted into the production group under the name *digit*? An error can arise in this production, if the current character is not a digit. However, one should take into account that both decimal point and semicolon are among admissible characters of the grammar.

Number is specified in the next group of productions. The error can arise, if the sentence is not a number or contains some characters which differ from digits. Since the nonterminal *number* is not a starting character as in the previous group, the nondigital current character will cause parsing to be continued in accordance with the nonterminal *decimal*. Now we have to discuss only the erroneous situation for a number of more than five digits. The text of the information message, i.e. 'number contains more than five signs', is placed in an appropriate production with the name number. Analogous comments concerning erroneous situations are assigned to the production decimal. The sentence containing the number of more than five digits will be provided with two messages: 'number contains more than five digits' and 'sentence is not a decimal number'.

Debugging language syntax takes place after the generator of language processors has started and a module of syntax analyzer in Pascal has been obtained. The given module is put together with the control program which calls in the former for execution. Some errors brought about by an incorrect record in metalanguage are announced in the process of generation. The errors resulting from inconsistency of the grammar with the language developed are revealed during the checkout of the processor, which contains the verified sentences of a language. These errors, when found out, require that the program in metalanguage should be corrected. Then the process recurs.

Semantics' arrangement and its interrelationship with the production elements is specified in metalanguage. The main principle implies that the semantic fragment should be performed right after the element of the production has been operated on when parsing. In the example of p. 147, the fragments

CIFRA := 0; and CHISLO := CIFRA; NUMBER := 1; will be executed after the character 0 on the input tape and the first digit of the number are admitted. Figure 4.1 shows the state graph for which the first fragment is assigned to the edge loaded with 0, the second to the edge loaded with *e*2, 2. It is recommended that semantics be assigned to the terminals of the productions.

Let us examine the production

CHISLO # ⟨CHISLO⟩⟨CIFRA⟩ # ⟨CIFRA⟩

with semantic fragments as shown in Fig. 4.1. The analysis of the state graph matching this production implies that the first and the only transition will take place along the edge loaded with *e*2. 2., the next transitions will occur along the edge loaded with *e*3, 2.. . Therefore, first, the program fragment

CIFRA#'a'

CHISLO#<CHISLO><CIFRA>#<CIFRA>

$\underbrace{\qquad}_{S1}$ $\underbrace{\qquad}_{S2}$

S1 → P:CHISLO:=CHISLO*10+CIFRA;
         NUMBER:=NUMBER+1;
S2 → P:CHISLO:=CIFRA;
         NUMBER:=1;

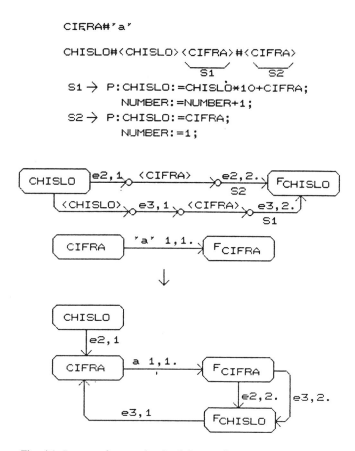

Fig. 4.1. Layout of semantics for left recursion

S2 will be performed once, and then the fragment S1 will be operated on. The same conclusion can be derived from the analysis of the production form. The only substitution causes the production # ⟨CIFRA⟩ to be involved. The production # ⟨CHISLO⟩⟨CIFRA⟩ is used $(n - 1)$ times for n substitutions taking place, where the element ⟨CIFRA⟩ corresponds to the fragment S1. Thus we get the following string:

$$⟨CHISLO⟩⟨CIFRA⟩⟨CIFRA⟩ \ldots$$

The last n-th substitution will replace the nonterminal CHISLO with the nonterminal CIFRA together with the semantic fragment S2. Therefore the fragment S2 contains the places allocated for the number being formed, and the fragment S1 is responsible for packing the current digit into a number.

On rearranging the nonterminals in the productions, let us consider the following sequence of productions:

$$\text{CHISLO} \# \langle \text{CIFRA} \rangle \langle \text{CHISLO} \rangle \# \langle \text{CIFRA} \rangle$$

Thus, we see that any of the nonterminals ⟨CIFRA⟩ can stand first. The number which consists of only one digit is associated with the fragment S2 being performed (Fig. 4.2). The *n*-digit number causes the fragment S1 to be per-

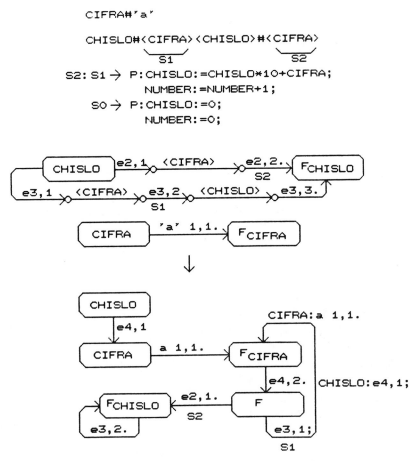

Fig. 4.2. Layout of semantics for right recursion

formed $(n - 1)$ times, and S2 to be executed once. On performing $(n - 1)$ substitutions, the string acquires the following form:

⟨CIFRA⟩ ... ⟨CIFRA⟩⟨CHISLO⟩

Such a sequence of performing the fragments follows from the analysis of the state graph constructed in accord with the given productions (Fig. 4.2). The fragments S1 and S2 are identical as they comply with the same conditions, and the initial statements S0 should be executed earlier, i.e. in the present case, at the outset of the parser and between the decimal point and the nonterminal ⟨CHISLO⟩, which belongs to the production group named *decimal*. Thus, the sequence of semantic fragments can be inferred from the production form.

Debugging the language processor proceeds routinely and employs all the methods applicable to the programs written in higher-level languages. The difference is that all changes are made in metalanguage, and the translation from metalanguage into higher-level language, i.e. Pascal, is automatic.

We have considered the characteristic properties of metalanguage which are substantial in language processor design. To illustrate the above-stated, let us develop a processor operating as a calculator.

4.4.   An Example of a Parser

Let us develop a program simulating the calculator provided with memory to show the applicability of the metalanguage and the language processor generator. The program represents some simple language processor intended for parsing and calculating ordinary arithmetic expressions. Compare the language processor being designed with the program in Pascal operating identically [15].

We are going to represent the program written in metalanguage by groups of productions, each provided with explanations,

SEXP / * initial grammar character */

*

ST : = 1;

⟨EXP⟩

MEMORY := EXPRESSION [ST];
WRITELN (EXPRESSION [ST]);

\# ⟨SEXP⟩
′,′

      ST := 1;
⟨EXP⟩

      MEMORY := EXPRESSION [ST];
      WRITELN (EXPRESSION [ST]);

The source sentence presents the expressions set off by comma from each other. The stack EXPRESSION with the pointer ST is employed for current calculations. The initial value of a pointer is equal to 1. At the outset of calculations the grammar with the * dummy character is complemented to enable the introduction of the initial character. The final result of calculations is held in the first stack element EXPRESSION [1]. The result of processing the expression is saved in MEMORY.

      EXP /* calculating the expression */
\# ⟨SU⟩

      EXPRESSION [ST] := SUMMAND [ST];
\# ⟨EXP⟩
′+′
⟨SU⟩

      EXPRESSION [ST] := EXPRESSION [ST] + SUMMAND [ST];
\# ⟨EXP⟩
′-′
⟨SU⟩

      EXPRESSION [ST] := EXPRESSION [ST] – SUMMAND [ST];

The expression can include either the only summand or the set of summands with pluses or minuses inserted between. On calculating the expression, the result is held in the stack element EXPRESSION [ST]. The outcome of calculations performed in parsing the summand is saved in SUMMAND [ST]

      SU /* calculating the summand */
\# ⟨MU⟩
      SUMMAND [ST] := MULTIPLIER
\# ⟨SU⟩

```
' * '
⟨MU⟩
              SUMMAND [ST] := SUMMAND [ST] * MULTIPLIER;
# ⟨SU⟩
' / '
⟨MU⟩
              SUMMAND [ST] := SUMMAND [ST] / MULTIPLIER
```

The grammar implies that the summand can be represented by a factor or some (of them) with either the multiplication or division signs inserted between. As already mentioned, the summand value is held in SUMMAND [ST]. The factor value is assigned to the variable MULTIPLIER.

```
              MU /* Parsing and calculating the factor */
# *
              FL := 0;
⟨NUM⟩
              IF ⟨ ⟩ 0 THEN FOR I := 1 TO PLACES DO NUMBER
                       := NUMBER / 10;
              MULTIPLIER := NUMBER;
# 'M'
              MULTIPLIER := MEMORY;
# '('
              ST := ST + 1;
⟨EXP⟩
')'           MULTIPLIER := EXPRESSION [ST];
              ST := ST - 1
```

A decimal number, a value of the previous expression held in MEMORY, and an expression parenthesized can be a factor. On parsing the factor, the result is assigned to the variable EXPRESSION.

The decimal number is calculated without consideration of the decimal point in parsing the production group named NUM. The result is assigned to the variable NUMBER. The position of the decimal point is defined by the number of decimal places following the point, which is held in the variable PLACES. The presence of the decimal point is associated with the flag FL. If the flag is not equal to zero, then the fractional part is present in the number. The given fragment transforms the number in consistence with its fractional part.

While computing the expression parenthesized, the bracket, once opened, increases the stack pointer as processing of the new expression starts. However, the outcome of the previous calculations may be requested later on. Reckoning the value of the expression parenthesized produces a factor which can be assigned to the variable MULTIPLIER. The stack pointer then decreases and the current value of the expression calculated before becomes available.

```
              NUM /* Parsing decimal number */
# ⟨IN⟩
# ⟨IN⟩
'.'

              FL := 1;
⟨IN⟩
IN /* Parsing number */
# ⟨DIG⟩
              IF FL = 0 THEN
                      NUMBER := ORD (DIGIT) − ORD ('0')
              ELSE
              BEGIN
                      PLACES := 1;
                      NUMBER := NUMBER * 10 + (ORD (DIGIT)
                      − ORD ('0'))
              END;
# ⟨IN⟩
⟨DIG⟩
              IF FL = 0 THEN
                      NUMBER := NUMBER * 10 + (ORD (DIGIT)
                      − ORD ('0'))
              ELSE
              BEGIN
                      PLACES := PLACES + 1;
                      NUMBER := NUMBER * 10 + (ORD (DIGIT)
                      − ORD ('0'))
              END
```

Parsing the decimal number to some extent differs from the one given in the previous section. All the digits of the number are packed as an integer and the digits of the fractional part are counted.

```
                        DIG  / *  Parsing  digits  * /
# '0'
                        DIGIT  :=  '0';
# '1'
                        DIGIT  :=  '1';
# '2'
                        DIGIT  :=  '2';
# '3'
                        DIGIT  :=  '3';
# '4'
                        DIGIT  :=  '4';
# '5'
                        DIGIT  :=  '5';
# '6'
                        DIGIT  :=  '6';
# '7'
                        DIGIT  :=  '7';
# '8'
                        DIGIT  :=  '8';
# '9'
                        DIGIT  :=  '9'
```

Variable specifications are placed in a separate module. The generator of language processors translates the present program into Pascal, which is then saved as a separate module. The modules generated and the module of specifications are processed by the Pascal translator. Having involved the standard object module, the linkage phase produces the ready-to-use program for expressions. The entire sequence of generation operations is applied automatically until the load module of the translator is produced. The generator only requests the names of the initial grammar character and the module of variable specifications. The following string exemplifies an expression:

$$3.23 * 5.62 * (23.5 + 56.59 - 156.456) - 1568.2 + 2.2458$$
$$* (26.54 + 0.0015) + 12.5 * 0.25 - 1$$

To evaluate the efficiency of the generator, the above parser was compared with a similar program in Pascal [15]. The results are listed in Table 4.1.

The load module can be subdivided into two parts: constant, which is independent of the language type, and varying. The constant part of the program in Pascal consists of 1536 byte against 4608 byte of the varying part. The program generated contains 5120 byte in its constant part against 2560 byte of the varying one. Therefore, for the languages whose grammars sufficiently exceed the above mentioned (e.g. 15-20 times), the volume of the generated language processor will be half of the identical processor in Pascal. Other characteristics presented in Table 4.1 reveal that the amount of the source text of the language processor recorded in metalanguage is three-fold less (processing speed is 1.2 times higher) and the amount of the parser is 16 times less than in the program routinely composed in Pascal.

Table 4.1 Relative characteristics of parsers

Comparable characteristics	Program in Pascal	Program in metalanguage
Body of the source text of the syntax analyzer, symb.	3900	240
Body of the full source text of the parser, symb.	6000	2040
Load module's body, byte	6144	7680
Program processing capacity, s/page	0.42	0.34

5 Language Processor Generator for Microcomputer

The techniques suggested for constructing the state graphs and the applicability of the latter to parsing can be used to advantage of design of language processors and their generators. The present chapter deals with one of the first versions of the language-processor generator. It can be interpreted as extension of Pascal by means of computer-aided design of parsers.

5.1.   Duty and Structure of the Generator

The generator promotes automatic development of the translators intended to process programming languages, conversations, problem-oriented languages, etc. The language design proceeds from its formal grammar and semantic description. The source translator should be recorded in the metalanguage considered above with its semantics presented in the form of the sentences written either in special macrolanguage or in Pascal. The outgoing ready-to-use translator is represented in some programming language (Fig. 5.1).

The generator consists of three programs: the program constructing the state graph, the program reducing the graph to its deterministic form, and the macrogenerator. The first program is responsible for preprocessing the translator being developed. Proceeding from the information on the grammar, the program creates the state graph, constructs the graphs for separate automatons of the system, and performs three transformations of the graphs described in Sections 2.1 and 3.1. The sentences containing language semantics and diagnostic messages are isolated into separate information blocks which will be exposed to the macrogenerator. Each diagnostic message and semantic fragment start with a mark. The descriptions of the edge loads of the state graph are provided with identical marks. The state graph is described in macrolanguage in the form of a character-coded text. See Appendix 2 for its grammar.

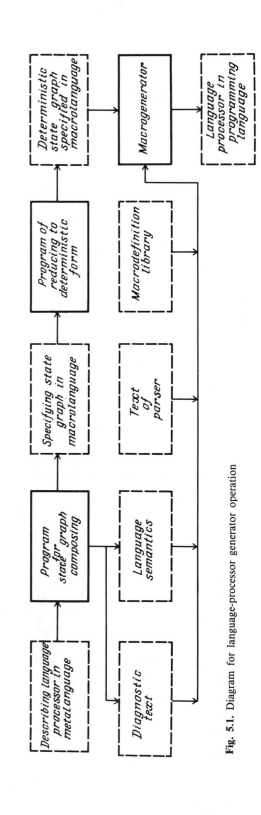

Fig. 5.1. Diagram for language-processor generator operation

The program reducing the state graph to its deterministic form analyzes the graph, reveals the vertexes where the selection of edges is ambiguous, and performs appropriate transformations (see Section 2.4). The deterministic state graph is also represented in the form of some text in macrolanguage. Representing the state graph's structure in the form of a text avoids the use of above programs for language processor design.

The state graph with the appropriate diagnostics and language semantics and the text of the parser enter the macrogenerator, which involves the macrodefinition library and performs translation from the macrolanguage into a programming language. A parser is a program scanning sentences of the language in accord with the expressions (3.8) through (3.12) specifying the change of configurations for some control unit. Let us discuss in more detail the macrolanguage subset used to specify the state graph (see Appendix 2).

The language specifying the state graph. The state graph shown in Fig. 3.3 will help us examine the instruction set of this language. The state graph description is subdivided into fragments. The fragment contains the specification of the edge group incident out of the same vertex. The state graph of Fig. 3.3 comprises twelve edge groups named after the vertexes they left. The vertex name preceding the group specification is followed by the information concerning each edge in particular.

The state graph contains both starting and end vertexes. The starting vertex name begins with the characters F:, and of the end vertex — with the characters L:.

F: S # / * starting vertex name */
. . .
L: FS # / * end vertex name */
. . .

The edge specification starts with the # character and presents either a comment or the full load of the edge, i.e. both right- and left-hand contexts, predicates, and the end vertex name. The left- and the right-hand contexts are marked respectively by the characters L: and R: on the left and by E on the right. A context comprises a series of nonterminals and chains of terminals. The former are enclosed in corner brackets, the latter are put in sparks. For instance

F: B # L : 'then' E . . .
 # L : 'begin' E . . .

The load of the edge undergoes no changes when transferred to its specification except for complementing it with semantics. The simple predicate presents either a chain of terminal characters put in sparks or a space character (*) followed both by the route and edge numbers, the flag of the last edge on the route (.), and semantics, set off by commas from each other. Semantics can be absent. The full load of an edge includes a series of simple loads separated by semicolon. Some vertex name can precede the simple load. The load can be either parenthesized or put in square brackets. The load parenthesized may recur infinitely, but once enclosed in square brackets implies that the first simple load of the sequence should be selected. Thus the meaning of notation used in constructing the state graph is valid in the language. For instance,

F:B # L: 'then' E * 14,1 N:M141 / * semantic label
       M141 */

F:C #
   # L: 'begin' E * 6,1 F:C

See Appendix 2 for full description of syntax for all the constructs. The description of the state graph of Fig. 3.3 recorded in macrolanguage is as follows:

```
/* ─────────────────────────────────────────────────────── */
    BEGIN:S #                                  'begin' 1,1 F:P
/* ─────────────────────────────────────────────────────── */
    F:P #                          *              2,1 F:B
/* ─────────────────────────────────────────────────────── */
    F:B # L: 'then'  E            *             14,1 F:C
        # L: 'begin' E            *              6,1 F:C
        # L: 'else'  E            *              9,1 F:C
        # L: ';'     E            *              5,1 F:C
        #            'if'                        4,1 F:A
/* ─────────────────────────────────────────────────────── */
    F:D #                          *             12,1 F:C
/* ─────────────────────────────────────────────────────── */
    F:C #                          *             10,1 F:A
/* ─────────────────────────────────────────────────────── */
    F:A #                         'i'            8,1. F:FA
        #                         'a'            7,1. F:FA
/* ─────────────────────────────────────────────────────── */
    L:FA #                         *             10,2. F:FC
         #                         *             11,2. F:FC
         #                        'then'          4,2  F:B
/* ─────────────────────────────────────────────────────── */
```

```
/ * ────────────────────────────────────────────────── */
      L:FC  #                    ':='           14,2  F:D
            #                    ':='            9,2  F:D
            #                    ':='            6,2  F:D
            #                    ':='            5,2  F:D
            #                    '+'            13,1  F:C
            #                     *             12,2. F:D
            #                     *             13,2. F:D
            #                     *             11,1;
                 A:              'i'             8,1. F:FA
            #                     *             11,1;
                 A:              'a'             7,1. F:FA
/ * ────────────────────────────────────────────────── */
      L:FD  #                     *             14,3. F:FB
            #                     *              9,3. F:FB
            #                     *              5,3. F:FB
            #                     *              6,3. F:FB
/ * ────────────────────────────────────────────────── */
      L:FB  #                     *              2,2. F:FP
            #                     *              4,4. F:FB
            #                   'else'           4,3  F:B
            #                    ';'             3,1  F:B
/ * ────────────────────────────────────────────────── */
      L:FP  #                     *              3,2. F:FP
            #                   'end'            1,2. F:FS
/ * ────────────────────────────────────────────────── */
      LAST:FS  *
```

The initial and the end grammar vertexes are respectively labelled with the key words BEGIN and LAST. So far as the language is not provided with specification for overlapping vertexes, three edges have been introduced (PB), (DC), (CA), loaded respectively with $e2$, 1, $e12$, 1, $e10$, 1. This caused the edge numbers of the paths 2, 10, 12 to be increased by one.

Though the language discussed above is intended for internal representation of the state graph, it can readily be adapted to design a language processor ignoring the graph's development and transformation programs. In what follows this language will be used in specifying the operation algorithms of the generator. To employ the generator, the user should have a deep insight into the subject. Therefore, let us consider the interface for one of the first versions of a generator. Its structure is nearly identical to the one shown in Fig. 5.1 but the former does not use a macrogenerator.

The parser generator GENER converts the translator in metalanguage into those in Pascal and macroassembler. In the course of generation it is recorded into the files of syntax tables (state graph) and semantics. The file of syntax tables is generated in macroassembler. The semantics file is generated either in Pascal or macroassembler depending on the language, in which the semantics has been recorded.

The generator is called by the monitor instruction RUN GENER. The request of the generator ENTER MODE requires that 1 or 0 should be keyed in via keyboard. Enter 0 to display the results of parsing, and 1 to file the listing into SYSOUT. PAS resides on the logic unit DK:. In this case only the erroneous sentences are displayed, showing the first eight incorrect characters indicated.

The next request SPECIFY PROGRAMMING LANGUAGE requires that the language used to record semantics of the translator being developed should be specified. Enter 0 for macroassembler and 1 for Pascal.

Type the source translator name to grant the request INPUT FILE NAME. Note that the present realization implies that the name of the input file should be identical with the initial grammar character. The output of the generator is saved in the file under the typed name to grant the request OUTPUT FILE NAME.

The generator produces the syntax tables in the form of a program in macroassembler and files them under the name of the initial grammar character with the extension .MAC. Labels are automatically assigned to semantic fragments and are gathered in one file. The labels facilitate binding the fragments to the syntax tables. Semantic file name is generated as follows: the first three letters of the file name are identical with those of the initial grammar character. The last letters are SEM. For example, the initial grammar character TABDEF corresponds to the file name TABSEM. Semantics recorded in Pascal or macroassembler are associated with either .PAS or .MAC extension of the semantic file name.

The two generated files should undergo translation. Call in Pascal translator for semantics written in Pascal:

      RUN PASCAL
        * semantic-file-name-DCLGB, semantic-file-name

where DCLGLB is the name of the file containing the specification of the variables met with in semantics. The output program is then subjected to macroassembler translator.

      RUN MACRO
        * semantic-file-name-semantic-file-name

* tables-file-name-tables-file-name
* ^C

The completed translator comprises the object modules produced and the constant object module MACNRB.OBJ. They can undergo editing together with some program calling in the translator generated.

Calling the translator written in macro assembler. The generated translator can operate in two modes. In the first mode, the source text is composed of a set of short sentences. Parsing each sentence requires calling in the translator. The second mode considers the whole program as source sentence. Let us discuss the first mode, where the sentences are no longer than five hundred bytes. Call in the translator: JSR PC, INITM. The input data are: R0, the address of the word containing the initial grammar character; R1, the address of the first character of the source sentence; R2 = 0 specifies the syntax analysis mode, R2 = 1 specifies the full parsing with processing semantics; R3 is the length of the source sentence.

The first call requires that some storage be allocated for stacks and their initial addresses be assigned to the variable STEKAS (STEKAS:: .WORD 0). The caller should specify global characters, e.g. .GLOBL INITM, XXXXXX where XXXXXX is an initial grammar character. On parsing the sentence, the translator sends the completion code to the register R3. If there are no errors R3 = 0, or else R3 ≠ 0. The error if revealed causes the address of the first incorrect character to be placed in register R1.

Let us consider the second case of calling the translator generated, i.e. when one deals with the sentence of undefined length: JSR PC, MGEN. The input data are: R0, the address of the word containing the initial character, R1, the address of the first character of the source sentence (i.e. its first string); R2 = 0 specifies the syntax analysis mode, R2 = 1 specifies the full parsing mode; R3 is the length of one string of the source sentence. The first call requires that the stack address must be assigned to the variable STEKAS. On parsing the string, the register R3 holds the completion code. After normal processing of all the strings of the sentence is complete, the program PROVST should be called in and the address R0, i.e. the address of the word containing the initial grammar character, should be specified. On executing the given program, the register R3 also holds a completion code. The code R3 = 0 implies that the source sentence contains no errors. To provide correct processing, the caller should specify the following global characters:

GLOBL MGEN, PROVST, XXXXXX

Calling the Pascal translator. The present instantiation of the generator employs some special procedure to call the translator generated. The procedure calls the translator from the main Pascal program as a subroutine.

> PROCEDURE PXXXXXX (STROKA: INTYPE; VIPSEM,
>   DLINA, PRIZNAK: INTEGER; VAR KOD: INTEGER;
>   VAR STRER: ERTYPE);
>   TYPE INTYPE = ARRAY [I..81] OF CHAR;
>   TYPE ERTYPE = ARRAY [I..81] OF CHAR;

where XXXXXX is the initial grammar character.

Let us consider both input and output procedure parameters for the sentence of finite length: STROKA is the source sentence; VIRSEM = 0, parsing mode, VIRSEM = 1, the full parsing mode; DLINA is the length of the source sentence; PRIZNAK = 1 implies parsing the whole sentence. Normal completion of the procedure corresponds with KOD = 0. The errors revealed are associated with KOD ≠ 0, that makes the variable STRER contain the first eight incorrect characters.

The second case deals with parsing a sentence of undefined length and matches the following parameters: PRIZNAK = 0, STROKA is a current string of the source sentence, VIPSEM is analogous to the previous case, DLINA is the length of the current string. On returning from the procedure, the completion code is assigned to KOD and the variable STRER is filled in as in the previous case. Normal completion of processing of all the strings of the current sentence demands that the procedure be finally called with the following input parameters: VIPSEM is equal to 0 or 1; PRIZNAK = 2, i.e. the flag of final call of the procedure; STROKA and DLINA take on arbitrary values. After termination of the procedure, the completion code value is set-in the variable KOD. KOD = 0 implies that the source sentence was incorrect.

Note that if the user is satisfied with the standard translator configuration, a command file GENV1 or GENV2 should be started. Its input includes the text of the translator written in metalanguage. The output contains the load modules of the translator filed by the name of the initial grammar character. When processing, the translator generated requests the name of the source file, where the original text is saved. If the original text is represented by one sentence, the instruction file GENV2 should be involved in generation, otherwise use GENV1. Thus using the generator of language processors is rather easy. Let us discuss its basic operation algorithms.

5.2. Operation Algorithms

The generator of language processors can operate according to three basic algorithms intended for constructing a state graph, parsing sentences of a language, and reducing a state graph to its deterministic form. All the algorithms proceed from the approach suggested in Chapters 2 and 3 for language processor design. Let us consider the algorithms in the above-stated order.

The algorithm of constructing a state graph is implemented proceeding from the three transformations discussed in Chapter 3. In the course of transformations, the grammar description recorded in metalanguage is converted into the state graph in macrolanguage. To illustrate the sequence of conversions performed consider the grammar of parsing the expressions given in Chapter 1.

$$E \to T \mid E + T \mid E\text{-}T$$
$$T \to F \mid T \times F \mid T/F$$
$$F \to a \mid \quad b \quad \mid (E)$$

The grammar described in metalanguage is taken as source information. To clarify the operations performed on semantics, let us put it down as labels on two terminal edges.

```
E  #  ⟨T⟩
   #  ⟨E⟩
      ' + '
              N:PLUS ⟨T⟩
   #  ⟨E⟩'-'⟨T⟩
T  #  ⟨F⟩  #  ⟨T⟩ ' × '  ⟨F⟩  #  ⟨T⟩ '/'  ⟨F⟩
F  #  'a'
      N:DIGIT
   #  'b'  #  '('⟨E⟩')'
```

The algorithm of constructing the state graph is obtained as follows.

1. Insert the dummy terminal into the right-hand parts of productions in the following cases.

(a) Let the mentioned character precede the nonterminal if the latter stands first in the right-hand part of the production and its name differs from that of the nonterminal in the left-hand part. In presence of the left context or some comment, the dummy character should be placed after them.

(b) The dummy character should be inserted between two adjacent nonter-minals if the second symbol is the last grammar character. In this case the character inserted will precede semantics, diagnostics and comments. Let us perform the first step for the above example.

```
E # * ⟨T⟩ *
# ⟨E⟩
' + '
            N:PLUS ⟨T⟩ *
# ⟨E⟩ '-' ⟨T⟩ *
    T # * ⟨F⟩ * # ⟨T⟩ '/' ⟨F⟩ * # ⟨T⟩ '/' ⟨F⟩ *
    F # 'a'
        N:DIGIT
        # 'b' # '(' ⟨E⟩ ')'
```

2. Denote the vertexes as in the case of macrolanguage. Consider the non-terminals from left-hand parts of productions as starting vertexes. Label them on the left with the characters F:. Put every initial node in correspondence with the final one. Its name is derived by complementing the initial vertex name with the character @. Place the end vertexes at the end of every produc-tion group and mark them with the character L: . Assign the characters BEGIN: and LAST:, respectively, to the initial and the final grammar characters.

```
BEGIN:  E # * ⟨T⟩ *
            # ⟨E⟩
            ' + '
                N: PLUS ⟨T⟩
            # ⟨E⟩ '-' ⟨T⟩ *
    LAST:  @E #
    F:   T   # * ⟨F⟩ * # ⟨T⟩'×'⟨F⟩ * # ⟨T⟩ '/' ⟨F⟩ *
    L:   @T  #
    F:   F   # 'a'
            N: DIGIT
            # 'b' # '(' ⟨E⟩ ')'
    L:   @F  #
```

3. Place a reference to an appropriate vertex after each terminal or dummy character. The reference comprises the characters F: followed by the name of

the nonterminal. The reference should be put down if the terminal precedes the nonterminal or the latter is the last grammar character. In the first case the reference name takes on the nonterminal name in the second case, it is identical with the name of the given group.

```
BEGIN:  E  # * F:T ⟨T⟩ * F:@E
            # ⟨E⟩
            ' + '
                N: PLUS F:T ⟨T⟩ * F:@E
            # ⟨E⟩ '-' F:T ⟨T⟩ * F:@E
LAST: @E #
  F:   T   # * F:E ⟨F⟩ * F:@T
           # ⟨T⟩ '×' F:F ⟨F⟩ * F:@T
           # ⟨T⟩ '/' F:F ⟨F⟩ * F:@T
  L:   @T #
  F:   F   # 'a'
                N: DIGIT F: @F
           # 'b' F:@F
           # '(' F:E ⟨E⟩ ')' F:@F
  L:   @F #
```

4. Assign ordinal numbers to all the right-hand parts of productions. Assign numbers to all the terminal and dummy characters of the right-hand part. The last character is always followed by a point. The numbers of productions and characters are separated from each other by commas. The numbers should follow immediately after the characters. Use the # character to separate the right-hand parts of the productions into elements corresponding to the edges. The # character follows each nonterminal.

```
BEGIN:  E  # * 1, 1F:T ⟨T⟩ # * 1, 2.F:@E
            # ⟨E⟩
            # ' + ' 2, 1
                N: PLUS F:T ⟨T⟩ # * 2, 2. F: @E
            # ⟨E⟩ # '-' 3,1F:T ⟨T⟩ # * 3,2.F:@E
LAST: @E #
  F:   T   # * 4,1F:F ⟨F⟩ # *4,2.F:@T
           # ⟨T⟩ # '×' 5,1F:F ⟨F⟩ # *5,2.F:@T
           # ⟨T⟩ # '/' 6,1F:F ⟨F⟩ # * 6,2.F:@T
  L:   @T #
```

```
F:   F   # 'a' 7,1.
              N: DIGIT  F:@F
         # 'b' 8,1.F:@F
         # '(' 9,1F:E ⟨E⟩ # ')' 9,2.F:@F
L:   @F  #
```

5. Delete the nonterminals and rearrange the edges. On deleting the nonterminal character the symbol ⟨X⟩ following the next edge if it is present, reset at the vertex L:@X. The edges bearing only the # character should be deleted at the vertexes which have more than one edge.

BEGIN:	E	#	*	1,1	F:T
LAST:	@E	#	'+'	2,1	
				N:PLUS	F:T
		#	'-'	3,1	F:T
		#	')'	9,2.	F:@F
F:	T	#	*	4,1	F:F
L:	@T	#	*	1,2.	F:@E
		#	*	2,2.	F:@E
		#	*	3,2.	F:@E
		#	'/'	5,1	F:F
		#	'/'	6,1	F:F
F:	F	#	'a'	7,1.	
				N:DIGIT	F:@F
		#	'b'	8,1.	F:@F
		#	'('	9,1	F:E
L:	@F	#	*	4,2.	F:@T
		#	*	5,2.	F:@T
		#	*	6,2.	F:@T

Having performed the given transformations, obtain a structure of the state graph of the source grammar described in macrolanguage. The first four transformations can be performed in single scanning of the source text recorded in metalanguage. The obtained graph is suitable for parsing.

The parser's algorithm simulates the change of configurations given by expressions (3.8) through (3.12).

1. Set the control unit into its initial state. Let the initial vertex labeled with the word BEGIN in macrolanguage be the current vertex. Denote it by A. Record the source sentence onto the input tape. The first sentence character

denoted by x becomes its current character. Set the stacks containing the numbers of paths and edges into their initial states. The initial pointer values of the stacks M and D should be equal to 1, i.e. $i = 1$ and $j = 1$ for the stacks M and L, respectively. The stack ML intended to register the process of parsing is empty in its initial state. The set of contexts expected is also empty. The counter of the current edge is $k = 1$.

2. Examine whether the current edge is available for transition. The transition along the edge is possible if the configurations can be replaced for each element of the edge load. The element is represented as load specified in macrolanguage by the nonterminal ⟨predicate and semantics⟩.

2.1. Save the current states of all the stacks and the input tape.

2.2. Check the following conditions.

(a) The left context assigned to the edge is absent or is present in the form of the right substring of the stack ML in accord with the algorithm described in Chapter 3.

(b) The current character x on the input tape is identical to the character of the load or else the element of the load contains the dummy character.

(c) The edge number of the load element is equal to 1, or else the edge number is less by one than the current number held in the stack D and at the same time the path number assigned to the edge is equal to that held in the stack M.

(d) The current character x is consistent with the character expected in the set of right-hand contexts MR. The condition is satisfied if (i) the left-hand characters of the context expected are either x or $A[$ and the edge number is equal to 1; (ii) the left-hand characters of the context expected are either x or $]A$ and the edge is the last on the route; and (iii) the character assigned to the edge is either identical to the left-hand character of the context or dummy and the left-hand character of the context is $]$.

2.3. If any condition is satisfied, then the configurations for one element are changed. In other words, use is made of step 4. The change of configurations involves modification of stacks and the input tape.

(a) Shift the pointer on the input tape if the element contains nonempty character.

(b) If the edge number is equal to 1, then shift the pointers $i = i + 1$ and $j = j + 1$, and save both path and edge numbers in the stacks M and D. If the element contains the term y and the initial vertex B or some edge leaves this vertex, then record the characters $B [y$ ($y = e$ is admissible) on the right-hand side of the string ML, and delete the characters y and $A [$, if present, on the left of the strings of the set *MR*. If *B* is a final vertex, then substitute an appropriate initial vertex for it in the string *ML*.

(c) If the edge number of the given path has taken on its maximal value, decrease the pointers of the stacks *M* and *D* by 1, i.e. $i = i - 1$ and $j = j - 1$, append the characters *y*] *B* (*B* is the vertex pointed by the given element) on the right-hand side of the string *ML*, and delete the characters *y* and]*B*, if present, from the strings of the set *MR*.

(d) If the intermediate edge of the path is analyzed, then the edge number held at the top of the stack *D* should be increased by 1, and the character *y* once complemented on the right-hand side of the string *ML* should be deleted from the strings of the set *MR*.

2.4. Select the next load element and use step 2.2. If the element being analyzed belongs to the sequence enclosed in square brackets, then skip the elements till the end of the sequence; select the following element and use step 2.2. If the considered element precedes the parenthesis, then find the element located immediately after a corresponding open bracket and use step 2.2. On examining all the load elements, execute all semantic fragments (their addresses are included into the load) and follow the next step.

3. Set a new current state, i.e. find the vertex where the analyzed edge enters. If the vertex is final, the stacks *MR*, *M* and *D* are empty and all the characters of the source sentence have been scanned, then the sentence belongs to the language, and parsing should be terminated. Otherwise use step 2.

4. Check whether the element belonged to the sequence parenthesized and recovered the state of parsing, when the parenthesized element is first met with. Then skip it and use step 2.2 if the next element is present, or else operate on semantics and use step 3.

If the element checked is enclosed in square brackets and there are still some elements between it and the] bracket, use step 2.2 to analyze the next element. If the element is the last one enclosed in square brackets, then use the next step.

5. Take the next edge rising from the vertex for examination. If it exists, use step 2. If no edge is available for transition after examining all the edges rising from the given vertex, the source sentence is erroneous. Then print diagnostics and use step 1 to process the next sentence. Stop translation after the source text comes to an end.

Note that the present algorithm operates only in accord with the deterministic state graph. Let us consider the general algorithm for reducing the state graph to its deterministic form.

The algorithm intended for reducing the state graph to its deterministic form proceeds from the results shown in Section 2.4. We will not dwell on its lengthy description, but shall discuss the main points.

1. Set the flag of the vertex modification to zero; this implies that no transformations take place in the graph. Select the graph vertex for an analysis such that it corresponds to the initial grammar character. Henceforth we shall denote by A the vertex being examined.

2. Examine all the edges incident out of the node. Examine the vertexes pairwise to reveal if any one of the three traits of indeterminacy is present. Analyze the edges as follows.

2.1. If two edges (A, X) exist and their terminal or empty loads are identical, perform one of the transformations (see Figs. 2.25, 2.26, 2.27, 2.28, 2.29, and 2.42); as a result, we shall get one edge (A, X) (X can overlap with A). If A is a final vertex and $A = X$, arrange the edges in the order stated in Section 2.4 (see Fig. 2.30). Note that step Ia of the algorithm of constructing the state graph cannot give rise to the situations shown in Figs. 2.30 and 2.31. In performing transformations account must be taken of the presence of semantics and diagnostics, which are transmitted to the extensions of the edges deleted.

2.2. If two edges which cannot be selected unambiguously have dummy characters in their loads, the latter should be increased. If an edge is a loop placed in the end vertex, arrange the edges in an ordered fashion. The edge assigned to the left-recursive production will be first, then the edge-loop follows, the edge assigned to the nonleft-recursive production is last. The loads are increased as is shown in Figs. 2.24, 2.32, 2.33, 2.34, 2.35, 2.37-2.42. On transferring the load the name of the vertex from which the edge with the mentioned load has arisen is written before the load. The load is parenthesized if transferred from an edge to a loop.

2.3. When two edges arise from one and the same initial vertex and can be selected unambiguously, they can be replaced by one edge where the initial loads of both edges are put in square brackets (see Fig. 2.41).

2.4. If at least one transformation has been performed, set its flag to 1 and use step 2.1. If no transformation has been performed, enter the vertexes pointed out by the edges considered in this step into the list of vertexes to be analyzed and have not been considered yet. Follow the next step.

3. Choose the next vertex from the list and perform transformation 2. If the list of vertexes has been completely examined and the transformation flag is not equal to 0, use step 1 to repeat the analysis. Otherwise stop transforming the graph.

As all the transformations of the state graph are performed in macrolanguage, they can be executed both by using some program and manually. The latter is used in the initial stage of generator design. To ensure generator's portability, the above algorithm should be recorded in macrolanguage.

5.3.   Implementation of Language Processor Generator

As mentioned before, a generator is mainly intended for computer-aided design of formal language processors. Numerous components of real programming systems and various systems can be considered as translators. Syntax of programming and other languages implemented in design of such systems can be usually specified in the form of a formal grammar. That is why the generator's range of application is rather wide. The generator can be used to best advantage for processing a language. This scope of problems concerns development of compilers, interpreters, macrogenerators, converters, computer control-oriented programming systems, robot control systems and database management systems. Let us discuss the generator potentialities when extending real programming languages and developing numerical control systems.

Extending programming languages. As already mentioned, a generator helps to extend the applicabilities of programming languages to processing texts. Using the generator's portability, you can apply it to a language, if you are not satisfied with its text processing. On porting, this language includes all the metalanguage statements, and the generator becomes its preprocessor.

Development of macrogenerators for real programming languages. According to Mac-Hillrow [14], a higher-level language contains a good deal of possible manipulations on texts. Hence, the compiler of the language once complemented with some statements, can be employed as macrogenerator. Porting the generator helps to bring the language to metalanguage, if necessary. Such an extension of a language promotes the design of macrogenerators for any languages irrespective of their level and the means available for manipulations on texts. Note that the obtained macrogenerator is syntax-oriented.

This idea can be realized as follows (Fig. 5.2). The source program recorded in macrolanguage is first handled by the modified generator of language processors and then twice processed by the programming language compiler. The first process is meant for performing macrooperations and the second

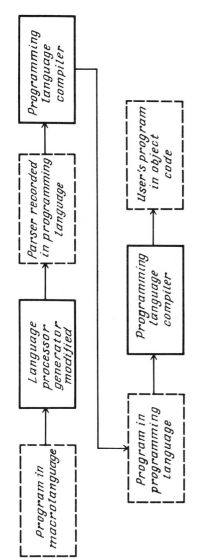

Fig. 5.2. Diagram for macrogenerator operation

for compiling the program generated in the first process. Obviously some procedures must be used to identify the programming language operators which are to be executed in the first process. This can be done by labeling the operators to be executed or ignored in the first stage. The latter is more preferable.

Generator modification consists in complementing it with some software which supports a number of transformations.

1. Semantic statements labeled as nonexecutable in the first process, take the form of the programming language sentences, which are then transferred to the output program generated.

2. The names of the variables met with in nonexecutable statements take on certain values while parsing is performed during first scanning. They are replaced with the values computed and sent to the outgoing text. If these variables are isolated in some way, the generator is modified insufficiently. Context replacing requires more complicated changes in the generator. Both modifications can be made without altering the real programming language.

This technique was employed for creating a PL/1 macrogenerator which was found to have the following advantages over the standard PL/1 macrogenerator called preprocessor.

1. The new macrogenerator is syntax-oriented.

2. Macrolanguage comprises the entire set of the language PL/1 compared to the preprocessor where this set is not complete.

3. The experiments have shown that macroprocessing is 40 times faster than a standard preprocessor.

Software development for numeric control systems. The software intended for analysis and parsing of control programs comprises series of translators of the languages describing workpieces, blanks, working technology, machine performance. These languages can be of different levels. Nevertheless, their syntax can be specified within formal grammars. Therefore, it is expedient to use the generator of language processors for developing formal grammars. Note that control programs can be parsed in real-time mode right during operation. Thus, the use of language multiprocessor will sufficiently decrease the operating time.

Using cross and resident computer programming systems promotes development of software for numeric control systems. The former usually consists of compilers, interpreters, composing and loading programs. Since all of them fall into translators, the use of a generator reduces their development time.

Thus, the fields of generator's application and its performance characteristics tell about its ample and advantageous implementation in the near future. Practically the scope of all the programming languages can be widened by using generators. Multiprocessing together with context-sensitive parsing and dynamic use of the generator enable efficient translators of new languages to be created. At present, the generators for Pascal and C-language have been implemented.

Appendix 1. Syntax of Metalanguage Describing Language Processors

To distinguish metalanguage from identical terminal characters we substitute metasymbol { } for ⟨ ⟩.

```
/* ——————————————————————————————— */
metalanguage /* Metalanguage describing language processors */
# {production group}
# {metalanguage} {production group}
/* ——————————————————————————————— */
production group
# {comment} {nonterminal} {production}
# {production group} {production}
/* ——————————————————————————————— */
production
# {comment} ” # ” {element}
# {production} {element}
/* ——————————————————————————————— */
element
# {left context} {comment} {predicate} {comment}
{semantics} {comment} {diagnostics} {comment}
{right-hand context}
# {comment}
/* ——————————————————————————————— */
semantics
# ”N:” {identifier}
# ”P:” {semantic characters}
# *
/* ——————————————————————————————— */
semantic characters
# {semantic character}
# {semantic characters} {semantic character}
/* ——————————————————————————————— */
predicate
# ” ’ ” {term chain} ” ’ ”
# ” ⟨ ” {nonterminal} ” ⟩ ”
# ” ⟨ ” {nonterminal} ” ⟩ ” {number}
# ” * ”
```

```
/* ──────────────────────────────────────────── */
number
#{digit}
#{digit}{digit}
/* ──────────────────────────────────────────── */
term chain
#{term}
#{term chain}{term}
/* ──────────────────────────────────────────── */
nonterminal
#{character}
#{nonterminal}{character}
/* ──────────────────────────────────────────── */
comment
#"/*"{comment characters}"*/"
#*
/* ──────────────────────────────────────────── */
comment characters
#{comment character}
#{comment characters}{comment character}
/* ──────────────────────────────────────────── */
left context
#"L:"{context}"E"
#*
/* ──────────────────────────────────────────── */
right context
#"R:"{context}"E"
#*
/* ──────────────────────────────────────────── */
diagnostics
#"//"{diagnostic characters}"//"
#*
/* ──────────────────────────────────────────── */
diagnostic characters
#{diagnostic character}
#{diagnostic characters}{diagnostic character}
/* ──────────────────────────────────────────── */
identifier
#{semantic character}
#{identifier}{semantic character}
/* ──────────────────────────────────────────── */
term
#{character}
#"/" #">" #"*" #"#"
/* ──────────────────────────────────────────── */
comment character
```

```
# {character}
#"/" #"⟩" #" #" #" ′"
```
/* —————————————————————————————————————— */
diagnostic character
```
# {character}
#"⟩" #" #" #" ′" #" *"
```
/* —————————————————————————————————————— */
semantic character
```
# {character}
#"/" #"⟩" #" *" #" ′"
```
/* —————————————————————————————————————— */
context
```
#"⟨" {nonterminal} "⟩"
#" ′" {term chain} " ′"
# {context} "⟨" {nonterminal} "⟩"
# {context} " ′" {term chain} " ′"
```
/* —————————————————————————————————————— */
character
```
#"A" #"a" #"B" #"b" #"C" #"c" #"D" #"d" #"E" #"e" #"F" #"f" #"G"
#"g" #"H" #"h" #"I" #"i" #"J" #"j" #"K" #"k" #"L" #"l" #"M" #"m" #"N"
#"n" #"O" #"o" #"P" #"p" #"Q" #"q" #"R" #"r" #"S" #"s" #"T" #"t" #"U"
#"u" #"V" #"v" #"W" #"w" #"X" #"x" #"Y" #"y" #"Z" #"z" #". " #, " #""""
#":" #"@" #"&" #"!" #"?" #" ̲ " #";" #"⟨" #"(" #"_" #"+" #"0" #"1" #"2"
#"3" #"4" #"5" #"6" #"7" #"8" #"9" #"[" #"]" #"{" #"}"
```
/* —————————————————————————————————————— */
digit
```
#"0" #"1" #"2" #"3" #"4" #"5" #"6" #"7" #"8" #"9"
```

Appendix 2. Syntax of Macrolanguage Describing State Graph

```
/* —————————————————————————————————— */
state graph
#{comment}{edge group}
#{state graph}{comment}{edge group}
/* —————————————————————————————————— */
edge group /* rising from the same vertex */
#{vertex name}" #"{edge}
#{edge group}" #"{edge}
# *
/* —————————————————————————————————— */
vertex name
#"F:"{nonterminal} /* initial vertex name */
#"L:"{nonterminal} /* end vertex name */
#"BEGIN:"{nonterminal}
#"LAST:"{nonterminal}

edge
#{left context}{comment}{load}{comment}
{diagnostics}{comment}{right context}
"F:"{nonterminal}
/* nonterminal — the next vertex name */
#{comment}
/* —————————————————————————————————— */
left context
#"L:"{context}"E"
# *
/* —————————————————————————————————— */
comment
#"/*"{comment characters}" */"
# *
/* —————————————————————————————————— */
load
#{predicate and semantics}
#{load}";"{predicate and semantics}
#"("{load}")"
#"["{load}"]"
```

```
{* —————————————————————— */
predicate and semantics
#{vertex}{left context}{predicate}
{semantics}{diagnostics}{right context}
/* —————————————————————— */
vertex
#{nonterminal}":"
#*
/* —————————————————————— */
predicate
#"'"{term chain}"'"{route number}", "{edge number}
{last edge flag}
#"*"{route number}", "{edge number}
{last edge flag}
/* —————————————————————— */
last edge flag
#"." #*
/* —————————————————————— */
route number
#{digit}
#{route number}{digit}
/* —————————————————————— */
edge number
#{digit}
#{edge number}{digit}
/* —————————————————————— */
semantics
#"N:"{identifier}
#*
/* —————————————————————— */
identifier
#{semantic character}
#{identifier}{semantic character}
/* —————————————————————— */
diagnostics
#"//"{diagnostic characters}"//"
#*
/* —————————————————————— */
right context
#"R:"{context}"E"
#*
/* —————————————————————— */
semantic characters
#{semantic character}
#{semantic characters}{semantic character{
/* —————————————————————— */
term chain
```

```
#{term}
#{term chain}{term}
/*  ————————————————————————————————————————————  */
nonterminal
#{character}
#{nonterminal character}
/*  ————————————————————————————————————————————  */
comment characters
#{comment character}
#{comment characters}{comment character}
/*  ————————————————————————————————————————————  */
diagnostic character
#{diagnostic character}
#{diagnostic characters}{diagnostic character}
/*  ————————————————————————————————————————————  */
term
#{character}
#"/" #")" #"*" #"#"
/*  ————————————————————————————————————————————  */
comment character
#{character}
#"/" #")" #"#" #"'"
/*  ————————————————————————————————————————————  */
diagnostic character
#{character}
#")" #"#" #"'" #"*"
/*  ————————————————————————————————————————————  */
semantic character
#{character}
#"/" #")" #"*" #"'"
/*  ————————————————————————————————————————————  */
context
#"⟨"{nonterminal}"⟩"
#"'"{term chain}"'"
#{context}"⟨"{nonterminal}"⟩"
#{context}"'"{term chain}"'"
/*  ————————————————————————————————————————————  */
character
#"A" #"a" #"B" #"b" #"C" #"c" #"D" #"d" #"E" #"e" #"F" #"f" #"G"
#"g" #"H" #"h" #"I" #"i" #"J" #"j" #"K" #"k" #"L" #"l" #"M" #"m" #"N"
#"n" #"O" #"o" #"P" #"p" #"Q" #"q" #"R" #"r" #"S" #"s" #"T" #"t" #"U"
#"u" #"V" #"v" #"W" #"w" #"X" #"x" #"Y" #"y" #"Z" #"z" #"." #", "
#""" #":" #"@" #"&" #"!" #"?" #"-" #";" #"⟨" #"(" #"_" #"+" #"0" #"1"
#"2" #"3" #"4" #"5" #"6" #"7" #"8" #"9" #"[" #"]" #"{" #"}"
/*  ————————————————————————————————————————————  */
digit
#"0" #"1" #"2" #"3" #"4" #"5" #"6" #"7" #"8" #"9"
```

REFERENCES

1. A. Aho and J. Ullman. *The Theory of Parsing. Translation and Compiling.* Vol. 1. *Parsing.* Englewood Cliffs, Prentice-Hall, 1972.
2. V.J. Rayward-Smith. *A First Course in Formal Language Theory.* Blackwell Scientific Publications, 1983.
3. O. Ore. *Theory of Graphs. American Mathematical Society Colloquial Publications.* Vol. 38. American Mathematical Society, Ahode Island, 1962.
4. A. Ollongren. *Definition of Programming Languages by Interpreting Automata.* London, Academic Press, 1974.
5. Ph. Lewis, D. Rozenkrantz, and R. Stearns. *Compiler Design Theory.* Reading, Addison-Wesley, 1976.
6. R. Hunter. *The Design and Construction of Compilers.* John Wiley and Sons, New York, Brisbane, Toronto, 1981.
7. V.N. Kasyanov and I.V. Pottosin. *Translator Constructing Methods.* Novosibirsk, Nauka Publishers, 1986 (in Russian).
8. V.M. Glushkov, G.E. Tseitlin, and E.L. Yushchenko. *Character Multiprocessing Approach.* Kiev, Naukova Dumka Publishers, 1980 (in Russian).
9. I.V. Velbitsky. *Programming Techniques.* Kiev, Tekhnika Publishers, 1984 (in Russian).
10. P.A. Timofeyev. *Design of Programs Intended for Identifying and Parsing Context-Sensitive Languages.* In: *Algorithmic Software and Design of Microprocessor Control Systems.* Moscow, MIET, 1982, pp. 39-50 (in Russian).
11. P.A. Timofeyev. *Parsing and Identifying Formal Languages.* In: *Design and Implementation of Control Systems on the Basis of Microprocessors and Minicomputers.* Moscow, 1983, pp. 67-75 (in Russian).
12. N.N. Mirenkov. *Parallel Programming for Parallel-Processing Systems.* Moscow, Radio i Svyaz Publishers, 1989 (in Russian).
13. *K.J. Terber. Architecture of High Throughput Computer Systems.* Moscow, Nauka Publishers, 1985 (Russian translation).
14. P. Brown. *Macro Processors and Techniques for Portal Software.* London, Wiley, 1974.
15. P. Grogono. *Programming in PASCAL.* Reading, Addison-Wesley, 1980.
16. V.F. Shangin, A.E. Kostin, V.M. Ilyushechkin, and P.A. Timofeev. *Programming of Microprocessor Systems.* (Ed. V.F. Shangin). Vysshaya Shkola, Moscow, 1990.
17. M. Sideris, *Inf. Process Lett.* 35, No. 2, 1990, pp. 103-109.
18. A. Bookstein, Sh.T. Klein, *ACM. Trans. Inf. Syst.* 8, No. 1, 1990, pp. 27-49.

INDEX